The Record Keeper

The Unfolding of a Family Secret in the Age of Genetic Genealogy

a memoir by

ALLISON LAWRENTZ BARNHART

Legacy Book Press LLC

Camanche, Iowa

*The Record Keeper: The Unfolding of a Family Secret
in the Age of Genetic Genealogy* by Allison Lawrentz Barnhart

Copyright © 2024 by ALLISON LAWRENTZ BARNHART

First printing, 2024

As it is with all personal narratives, this one is subjective.
This story is told from the author's perspective and her memories;
she recognizes that everyone remembers events differently.

ISBN: 979-8-9874823-9-1
Library of Congress Case Number: 1-13659182304

Cover Design by Allison Lawrentz Barnhart

Legacy Book Press, LLC.
1431 Hiawatha Lane
Camanche, IA 52730

www.legacybookpress.com

Printed in the United States of America

"*For now we see only a reflection as in a mirror;
then we shall see face to face. Now I know in part;
then I shall know fully, even as I am fully known.*"
1 CORINTHIANS 13:12

For Miles & Clementine

*May you stay curious about where you came from
and where you're going. And don't be afraid to
keep some records of the journey along the way.*

❧ contents

Allison & Jen (2019)

Debbie, Helen, Mike, Karen, Susie, Linda (2017)

Mike & Karen (1961)

(2003)
Back L-R: Frank, Jim, Mike
Front L-R: Linda & Evelyn

(1981)
Back L-R: Karen, Linda, Wilma, Sylvia;
Front L-R: Helen (& Jen!), Carol, Susie, Debbie

ACKNOWLEDGEMENTS

Grandma, thank you. This book is what poured out from years of wanting to understand more about you and about my family; it is my hope that it's a work that expresses honor and gratitude to all you taught me and to your anything but ordinary life that made our lives possible.

To my dad. Thank you for working hard for us and loving us well. For being an amazing grandpa to my kids and father-in-law to Jason, and husband to Mom. Thank you for showing me how to be curious and encouraging my creativity. Your perseverance and determination opened up countless opportunities for us to get involved in art, sports, music, to travel near and far, and try new things. Thank you for being willing to share your stories with me over the years and for being open to accepting a new story and allowing me to share it with others. I love you.

Thank you to Jen, who I'm indebted to for walking with me through this extraordinary journey I could have never imagined we'd be on. Without you, none of it would have been possible. And while I'm sad we had to wait until our 30s to even know of one another, I'm so grateful we know each other now. I hope you know how deeply treasured and loved you are.

Thanks to my Uncle Jim and Uncle Frank for your love, encouragement, and support for this project but also the ways you've added to my life. I'm blessed to have uncles that treat me like a daughter and allow my curiosity to venture down family history paths that occasionally have unexpected results!

Thanks to the Eckstrom sisters, my surprise/bonus aunts! For their generous acceptance, genuine warmth, and open hearts. It has been a joy to be a part of each of your families. You have ALL been a crucial part of helping Jen and I put the puzzle pieces together. There were traits and characteristics about myself, my sisters, and my dad that I was never quite sure where they came from—but after meeting you all, so much started to make sense! You were willing to get to know us when we were just strangers and share with us the family history we never knew we had been without. The doting, love, and concern you have shown my dad melts my heart. What a blessing it is to have you and your families in our lives.

To my mom, Mindy, for her constant encouragement and interest with my family history research and this project, showing me how to be a devoted wife, mother, daughter and daughter-in-law and cheering me on in all my endeavors and whims. I love you so very much, you are an incredible grandma and mom.

To my dear sisters Elizabeth Mikulandra and Samantha Lyons who were just as impacted by the discovery as I was, and who embraced the family and their inner Swede. I love you both.

Deep thanks for my grandparents who made such a positive impact in my life—Stan & Joan Scroggs; Evelyn & Pete Boreman. In memory of my late Aunt Linda Louise, who exuded gentleness, love, and family.

To my cousins Mandy and Emily who are like an extra set of sisters to me. Their support and encouragement mean the world to me and I'm blessed to call them family. They say that your cousins are your first friends, and that is true of how I consider you two.

Deep thanks to my friends and sisters in Christ, Anne Williams and Jillian VanDuyne. You have been loyal and constant encouragement, the truest of friends. I love you both, Anne with an "E" & Jilli!

To Jerry and Ellen for being so kind, helpful, and enduring my many questions and curiosities.

Thanks to our first neighbors and treasured friends Heather and Jayson.

To all who encouraged, listened, and gave welcomed advice, notably: Becca, Chad, Colleen, Daniel, Jared, Kimberly, Morgan, Sarah, and Sonja.

I am grateful to my publisher Jodie Toohey of Legacy Book Press, LLC for giving me this incredible opportunity to share my story to a wider audience and for the hard work and care she gives to helping her authors tell their tales.

A deep and sincere thanks to Mae who has been an invaluable part of my grandma's life and our family's story. I will never forget her kindness and willingness to share her memories and thoughts with me during that intense discovery period of time. Mae, thank you for helping me discover a more complete picture of who my grandma (and your long time best friend) was. You are a treasure. *Updated to add: Rest in peace, Mae.* 20 MAR 1928 — 04 FEB 2024

To Jason, for all the ways you care for me and our kids. I have a blessed life with you. Thank you for urging me to write my story. I love you.

PART I

CHAPTER 1

FORGET ME NOT

Spring, 1962

"All children, except one, grow up. They soon know that they will grow up, and the way Wendy knew was this. One day when she was two years old she was playing in a garden, and she plucked another flower and ran with it to her mother. I suppose she must have looked rather delightful, for Mrs. Darling put her hand to her heart and cried, 'Oh, why can't you remain like this forever!' This was all that passed between them on the subject, but henceforth Wendy knew that she must grow up. You always know after you are two. Two is the beginning of the end." [1]

He woke up to a sound coming from downstairs, something musical. Curious, he made his way down the old house's creaking steps. On the stairs you could slip and fall; the two-and-a-half-year-old knew that full well. He was determined he wouldn't let that happen a second time. Eventually he'd fall again, but not now. He remembered what could happen. Grasping the railing, he climbed slowly and carefully down to the first floor past the novelty plaque reminding all readers: *Shhh! Baby Sleeping.*

---

[1] J.M. Barrie, Peter and Wendy (New York: Charles Scribner's Sons, 1911; Project Gutenberg, February 15, 2021), https://www.gutenberg.org/cache/epub/16/pg16-images.html.

Though it was the middle of the night, the sweet lilting sound of a song had drawn the little boy from his bed and into the dimly lit dining room. Peeking between the curtain panels, the only light came from the streetlamps and found its way through the nearest window. On top of a China cabinet sat a round, aluminum music box, painted blue, playing "Waves of the Danube" waltz. Staring in the direction of the music, he didn't go near. Everything was still and quiet aside from the repeating melody coming from the music box. He knew there was no way to reach it—he was still too small.

Looking around, he realized he was alone. Everyone else in the family was still upstairs asleep in their beds. He made his way back up the steep staircase and crawled underneath his covers until morning. It was his first memory.

❧

May, 2017

Next to being confident in his smarts and quick wit, it's having a vivid recollection that Dad prides himself in. He could rely on it. Remembering and knowing is how he's built his life. It's even how he taught himself music—by ear, by memorizing.

I haven't been sleeping well. Lately, the words I say to him seem forced and hollow; I'm struggling to make eye contact when I'm around him, dreading that he knows I'm keeping a secret from him. Maybe he can't quite pinpoint what it is, but he knows it's something. If I wait much longer he might start reading my mind. That I've kept quiet even a couple days, let alone for two months is a miracle.

But *she* lasted well past a measly two months. She kept silent for *fifty years* until finding rest in the Lord. It's now my unexpected (and perhaps my unavoidable) inheritance. The secret found me and claimed me as its caretaker—whether I wanted the job or not.

Leave it alone, a thought had said. *What good will it do him if he knows?*

Maybe if I had just stopped, I could have let it go. I could have just kept it for her; like I had done with the knickknacks and Avon earrings and beads. I could just store the secret away in a sealed container. Her scrapbooks and postcards had met that time capsule-like fate along with the hundreds—maybe thousands—of photographs. The secret would be safe there. If someone else stumbles upon it in the future, so be it. Why should *I* be the one to open the door containing a giant family skeleton and get buried under a whole pile of miscellaneous bones that come tumbling after? There had to be a reason my grandmother took it to the grave.

Stop making excuses, another thought said. *You're trying to find a different way out when there is no other way.*

But there has to be, I pleaded.

If Dad is never told, will I regret it? Who am I to withhold his identity from him? He was named after a man who he believed was his father. As much damage as that man caused the family, it's been the shared surname and the lineage that exists beyond him that we've come to embrace as our own. Until now, there had been no reason to believe otherwise.

He sits down at the head of the table, placing both hands in front of him, stretching his long fingers out over the slight gap where the table pulls apart to make space for the leaf. Sitting down in a chair next to his, I run my fingers over the hieroglyphics of my youth, proof of my sisters' and my existence and of our elementary school math worksheets. The well-loved oak dining room table reveals the worn and faded spots of family life, which, despite the solid hardwood, feels oddly soft. This is the place where we have not only done homework, but eaten most every meal, dyed Easter eggs, decorated Christmas cookies, played board games, and blew out birthday candles year after year.

Reaching in my bag, I pull out a bottle of Mic Ultra and place it directly in front of him. He laughs and knows right away to be suspicious. His current reality is that he has three full siblings: the ones he's always known. In a matter of minutes, he'll know that's not the case. Adding seven half-siblings makes the grand total ten. Ten half-siblings his entire life, and a thousand unanswered questions for my dead grandmother.

Even with that steel trap of a memory he's depended on his whole life, he'll look at all the proof and he'll wonder why he can't remember *any* of it.

CHAPTER 2

WILL THE CIRCLE BE BROKEN

Spring, 2007

Now smaller in her polyester button-down shirt, my grandma greeted me at the door with a quiet "Howdy!" and ushered me in to "Sit down and stay a while, Honeychile." I had stopped by as planned with my camcorder, tripod, and an hour lunch break to interview her. Being interviewed wasn't the problem; it was being the center of attention for the camera that I knew bothered her. I tried to play it down as much as possible.

After a few recent conversations with her, it occurred to me she was slipping more and more with her stories from her youth and from when she was raising my dad and his siblings Linda, Jim, and Frank.

You should have done this years ago, I scolded myself.

With the camera running, we sat looking at family photos, mostly quiet but now and then she would utter commentary in her warm, meek voice. Her hair was thinning, but she styled it like she always had: parted on the left so most of her hair covered the indent on the top right of her forehead. With very little inflection, she commented on every other photograph or so.

"That one's your mom's dad, right? You want to give that to him?"

"That's so-and-so's little kid."

"They went and tore that building down now."

"Her and her daughter would bring me pants to hem."

"I wonder if he'll ever get married."

"Do you have a copy of this one?"

"Is this your sister?"

"That's the one out on Wells Road."

On playback, the image was grainy and the audio squeaky—you could hear the gears of the camera turning more than you could hear our voices. I wondered if her quietness and reservation was partly due to my noisy camera reminding us it was watching. My prehistoric digital camcorder sat on the tripod facing her, the red light on and recording as she flipped through small photo albums which were not in any kind of order, chronological or otherwise. The process of going through pictures together just to talk about them is something we did quite often—in fact, we did this whenever I came to visit. Of course, unless *Jeopardy* or *Gilmore Girls* were on.

She handed me a black and white photo of herself in a dress and smiled. "This is before we went to prom."

"Aww, that's pretty! Who'd you go with?"

"Oh, I can't think of his name off hand...just a friend of the family." I examined it a little longer as she thought.

"An...Ander...Anderson I think was his last name."

"What happened to your dress?" If there was a chance she kept any 1940s dresses or other vintage clothing I'd be over the moon.

"Well, I came to Ashland right after I graduated and took it to the cleaner. They ruined it. It was a white dress."

Photos I was very familiar with revealed a vibrant and free-wheeling young woman who seemed to morph into a subdued and controlled one with each passing year.

"Grandma, this is an odd question, but how old do you see yourself?" After a silent beat, I thought I might rephrase the question, but she spoke up. She understood what I meant.

"In my mind I'm still 16," she answered. And I knew what *she* meant—wondering how the years had snuck up on her and made a young girl into a grandmother. A great-grandmother, even.

"Did you ever wish you'd have learned to drive?"

"No, I don't think so. Getting stuck on the train tracks scared me too bad." She paused. "Once, though, when I was going with this one guy, we were driving from Ashland to Wooster. He pulled over and told me to get out. So I got out and he said to get in the driver's side, so I drove for just a little bit."

Evelyn LaRue Bowers was just LaRue to the Georgia relatives. Eventually, other nicknames followed: "Evie" and "Shorty." It'd be a stretch to say she collected nicknames with only three. But considering all her other growing collections, it became clear that she had a collection problem. A "problem" that was only really a problem for everyone else in the family. Finding the time to do what she wanted with it all was *her* real dilemma.

No one ever called her a hoarder to her face. They'd just say things like: "What are you going to do with this?" or "I think you already have one of those," or "Do you really need that?"

Rocks, mugs, autographs, magazines, dolls, coasters, placemats, buttons, coins, plastic Scope mouthwash caps, books, recipes, hair cuttings, empty cigarette cartons, teeth, postcards and postmarks, plastic bags, newspapers, newspaper clippings, the elastic waist bands from pairs of Fruit of the Looms, a brick from the old jail, costume jewelry, plastic canvases, scrap fabric, crochet patterns, Avon bottles, Cracker Jack toys, keychains, yarn and thread, stuffed animals, salt and pepper shakers, Styrofoam and plastic containers from restaurants, beads, coupons, knickknacks of all kinds, and a snowball from the blizzard of '78 (preserved in the freezer, naturally).

I never collected autographs like my grandma did, and though many of her more famous autographs were sold, she gave me one she still had in her collection. Frankie Goldsmith, a child survivor of the *Titanic*, lost his father in the disaster. After living in Detroit with his mother, he moved to the Ashland/Mansfield area and started a photo supply business.

One day, he had come into Gault Cleaners where Grandma worked downtown, and she recognized his name right away. One of the few things she wasn't shy about was requesting autographs and Mr. Goldsmith was no exception.

She saved the signed scrap of paper in a book called *The Sinking of the Titanic and Great Sea Disasters: Thrilling Stories of Survivors with Photographs & Sketches* (1912); it was published only a short time after the sinking in April of that year. Her father, Frank Bowers, had owned the copy. She knew I was drawn to the story since seeing a National Geographic special on the sinking and wanted me to have the fragile and yellowed book. Now I had my very own piece of *Titanic* history *plus* a survivor's autograph. Since we didn't have an ancestor who had been a passenger on the *Titanic,* it was the next best thing.

Grandma also took pictures. Which is a kind of collection all its own.

Pictures of clouds, flowers, rainbows, hot air balloons, spring leaves, summer leaves, fall leaves, gardens, large snowfalls, gifts, food, floral arrangements, people, animals, people with animals, people crying, people laughing, people smiling, people swimming, people riding bikes, people dressing up, people taking pictures, people eating, people playing instruments, people wearing wigs, people in open caskets, clowns, neighbors, her young sons dressed up like little girls, herself in a mirror, kids playing, parades, injuries, presents, fairs, road signs, funny signs, picnics, buildings being torn down, buildings being built, relatives' grave markers, humorous or interesting grave markers, landmarks, historical artifacts, places she used to lived, the TV when someone she liked or knew was on it, and lastly, pictures of pictures. She'd get doubles or triples made and make sure you got one if it involved you.

Within her quiet and accommodating demeanor remained a hopeful and curious girl, keeping a close eye on the world around her, attempting to collect and record her observations like a scientist of the natural world. But for her, the research was purely for the collecting and for the keeping.

Her scrapbooks are a circus of content. They are filled with the interesting, cute, funny, clever, and bizarre. Lined with clippings of movie stars and popular singers, weddings, and engagements of local couples as well as celebrities, photos and drawings of human and animal babies, and the occasional pressed flower or four-leaf clover. Comics and cartoons—even a few of her own drawings. Sad accidents or weird crimes committed locally and worldwide; even articles on the events of World War II, of classmates she knew who were killed in action or missing.

"Here's Mae and I at the Miller Street house." She handed me a loose black and white photograph tucked in between the pages of the next small photo album she placed on her lap. Sly smiles matched their smart bobbed hair, high heels, handbags, and corsages pinned on the upper left of their identical cropped swing coats.

Mae was a familiar figure in our family's story and a household name—no last name was needed when she was mentioned. In the mid 1940s, Grandma's parents still lived on the farm in Ashland County. Grandma Bowers' younger brother, Bob, who had moved up to Ashland from Georgia after his time in the war, was called upon to be a "taxi driver" to his slightly younger niece, Evelyn, when she was finished with high school back in Akron.

He was also kind enough to give the neighbor's daughter, Mae, a lift into town. Both being the same age, Evelyn and Mae became quick friends and an inseparable duo while Uncle Bob chauffeured them to their places of employment. Daily, Grandma was dropped off at Cresco, a men's garment factory which manufactured leather and cloth jackets and coats where she worked as a seamstress. Mae's daily stop was at the Ashland High School for office work. After learning to drive, she stopped catching rides with Bob and Evelyn, but the girls' friendship continued to grow.

Grandma wasn't as independent as I'm sure she'd thought she'd be when she was young. But Mae, on the other hand, was always very independent: she would go on to have a successful career while being a divorcee and single mom. In their retirement years, she would pick up Grandma on Tuesdays to go grocery shopping together. They fondly referred to it as "Mae Day."

While Mae never remarried, Grandma had divorced and remarried within the same year. It was 1966 and after seventeen years with Phil Lawrentz, she would meet and marry Donald Junior Boreman, better known to family and friends as Pete.

Evelyn and Pete went down to Winchester, Virginia, and made it official at the Justice of the Peace. I asked Grandma to retell the story to me for the camera.

"I remember going to the place that marries you—whatever you call it, and uh, I picked up something. I think it was a pinecone, or something from the tree there and he says 'C'mon! Let's get this blankety-blank thing over with. I'm getting hungry,'" she said with a smile that confused me.

Pete came into their lives as an alcoholic who, when drunk, became angry, jealous, and controlling. The autographs of famous people she'd been collecting for years? He sold them. Her diaries of life prior to him? He burned them. He moved Grandma and the kids to a new house and isolated them for a time. Even Mae was kept at a distance during those early years of their marriage.

Whenever I heard about those early "Petermo" days, he did not sound like the grandpa I grew up knowing, but I was always comforted by the knowledge the future held for him: a change of heart.

I started to wonder how dysfunctional cycles get started. Abuse, alcoholism, rage, workaholism, overeating, hoarding. What allows them to become part of a family's identity and story? And furthermore, I wonder what's exaggerated in these recollections grandkids like me get told—and what's left out altogether.

Grandma passed me a family photo and said, "You can have it. 'Cause when I die, somebody will say 'who's that?'" I guessed that to mean I could fill in the blanks when questions arose. But I was certain my dad's generation would help me out if I got stumped.

"Well, I hope strangers don't get your pictures."

"I do too."

Much like the contents of the many boxes piling up in her home, her stories were filled with bits of memories and random treasures from the past—never in much of any order.

She would gently set them out for me, like the pretty or interesting stones she collected: once part of a bigger rock, but nearly impossible to place back into its original form.

CHAPTER 3

DECONSTRUCTION

Summary, 2007

[LAWRENTZ FAMILY TREE]

LIDA Lawrentz — SYLVIA Clark

HARRIET EDNA BONNIE MILTON   DON JACK CLARENCE DOLLY PATTY JOHN

FRANK Bowers — GRACE England

RON HAROLD DALE

PHIL Lawrentz ——————————— EVELYN Bowers

LINDA   JIM   MIKE   FRANK

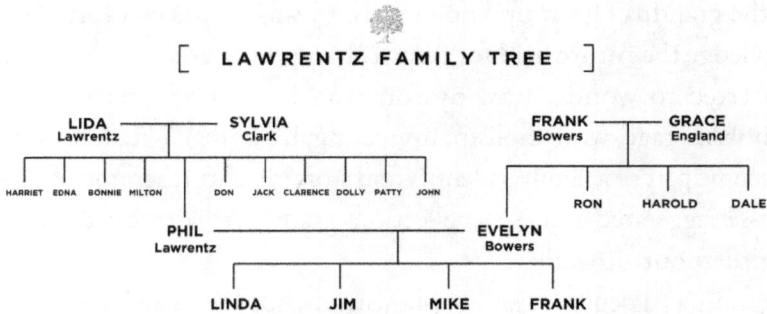

Not long after my video interview with Grandma, summertime brought an opportunity to see a piece of family history up close. My sister Sam and I drove the five hours south from Ashland to Spencer, West Virginia, a small rural town that wasn't really on the way to or from anywhere. All we knew was that a log cabin once belonging to the Lawrentz family remained on a few acres of land off of Missouri Fork Road. Our third great-grandfather Noah Lawrentz settled there along with his family after moving west from Lewis County, and prior to that, Fauquier County, Virginia.

Our parents and younger sister Elizabeth planned to join us later in the day. Once we had all arrived at the motel, we made our way out to the cabin site.

Growing up, our family had spent summers visiting historic landmarks across the country during past vacations, but this trip was different. This time we had a chance to personally connect with a historic site like we never had at The Corn Palace, Four Corners, or Wall Drug. It was no doubt a less popular destination, but the thought of seeing something from our heritage was unquestionably exciting to us.

> "Of upper Spring Creek. Noah Lawrence and his wife, Elizabeth (Allman), with the first born of their several children, five sons and two daughters, came here from their former home in Lewis or Harrison County about the year 1850. They were of the third or fourth generation of the Lawrences, early settlers of the Monongahela Valley; and came here and invested inheritances and savings in a large tract of land, virgin forest, on upper Spring Creek.
>
> The spelling of the name, Lawrence, appears on the county records in different letterings; the first deed of conveyance in this name is one by Alexander; to it he and his wife append their names spelled 'Lorentz'.
>
> Noah and his family were popular people in their part of the county for some twenty-five years." [2]

Along with the cabin, I learned (with the help of some distant Lawrentz cousins) there were stories beyond my estranged grandfather Phil we *could* be proud of—or were at least worth learning about. French and Indian War soldiers; victims and survivors of an Indian massacre; pioneers and members of the House of Burgesses in colonial Maryland. I pored over old records, military histories, ship passenger lists, and Google Earth views. Zooming in on land my ancestors cared for and were laid to rest on captured my imagination.

The old Lawrentz homestead appeared around the bend in the road. To our surprise, it was a demolition zone.

[2] The History of Roane County, 1927 (Roane County Historical Society, 1927).

We proceeded with caution and saw they were in the middle of tearing white aluminum siding off the home to reveal old timbers which hadn't seen the light of day in decades. Pink and yellow bits of insulation littered the ground like clouds of cotton candy sprinkled amid the gnarled pieces of siding, splintered off pieces of wooden trim and frames, and the odd scrap of tattered and frayed carpet.

With permission from the new owners (who happened to be nearby), we were able to walk inside and look around. Dad brought the camcorder and he and I took turns taking video as well as photos with a digital camera, trying to thoroughly document this rare piece of Lawrentz history. It gave me chills to think my ancestors lived in this very place, this humble home, taking the risk to move further west in those early days—pre–Civil War and before West Virginia knew statehood.

After we finished exploring the log cabin, we drove down the country road to find the old cemetery nearby on Missouri Fork and saw the first Lawrentz headstone I had ever seen in my life. Next, we attended a genealogical event in the town of Spencer and left feeling even more connected to our roots. I bought a Roane County Genealogical Society T-shirt to commemorate our visit.

"Maybe we can find a way to pool enough money together and buy this land back someday," said Dad proudly.

Months later, another distant Lawrentz cousin shared how the new owners of the land were very gracious to let him have the massive old beams of the log cabin for free. He meticulously numbered and kept track of each original wooden beam and would store them until he could reconstruct the home on a piece of land he owned elsewhere in West Virginia. He told me he'd let me know when it was rebuilt, and we'd plan a big family reunion.

That old cabin had been a tangible key to reimagining our heritage. We could now see what was underneath: a rich history, not a dead end.

Something ugly was covering it and kept it in the dark, but getting there at just the right time allowed us to see light hit the original structure. It was a symbol of who we were and where we came from.

CHAPTER 4

MY DEAR ACQUAINTANCE

Christmas, 2009

$\mathcal{S}$itting on my lap, Miles held Grandma's pointer finger tightly with his pudgy little hands. She had always loved babies.

"Mom, Ali, Bocephus, say 'cheese!'" Dad said, as he snapped a picture of us together. As soon as he found out he would be a grandpa, he started calling the kidney bean sized baby of mine "Bocephus."

Our family gathered in the visiting room at the Good Shepherd Home. Dad celebrated turning fifty the week before with a homemade fruit cocktail cake my mom made him—just like his mother used to make.

Since Grandma moved from her two-story house to the tiny ranch her parents had lived in for decades, things hadn't been the same for her. Sometime after Aunt Linda died in 2004, she would only sleep on her living room couch or a recliner and started eating less and less.

Though quiet, she had been a wonderfully social creature. But now in the old folks' home, she ate alone in her room. Her roommate annoyed her, and she didn't like participating in any resident activities. She hardly ate and was consistently stubborn about drinking enough water. When we saw her on Christmas, Grandma didn't say a word—her Parkinson's had progressed—but I could tell she enjoyed the interaction with my six-month old. By the next week and on Uncle Jim's birthday, she was gone. The last day of the year.

"Jason, we have to head back early." We began the eight-hour ride home from Virginia where we were visiting his family for the holidays. It felt much longer than eight hours. My mind obsessed over her: what I knew about her and all the things that were too late to discover. I wondered if she'd have an open casket. *She'd hate that,* I thought.

For more than 60 years, all the things she collected and recorded were moved from place to place, stuffed in boxes, laid in between books, and set aside. Indefinitely. Some of these were the stories only palatable at family gatherings; stories that got a consistent laugh. Others were the stories that seemed more like tall tales and made the elders in our families out to be nothing less than brave and heroic; still others were more like cautionary tales for children. What truth was in all of them, as with any family story, is hard to say.

Not being physically present for most tales, I'd rely on bits and pieces of memories and perspectives from various people in the family; the stories we think we know intimately sometimes end up more like acquaintances. What did I really know about any of it at all?

For the calling hours and funeral, I was asked to put together a slideshow. I remembered her telling me she loved Peggy Lee. She was also an avid Elvis, Eddy Arnold, and Johnny Cash fan. It would be hard to choose only one or two songs as a soundtrack of my grandmother's life.

Then the perfect song showed up in my search: "My Dear Acquaintance" (1960) performed by Peggy Lee. A song similar to the traditional New Years anthem "Auld Lang Syne", I knew Grandma would appreciate the significance of this selection.

After the funeral, I had a dream of a little girl with short hair playing outside in a neighborhood. Laughing and smiling, she pranced along the sidewalk until she found her tricycle. The scene was dimly lit, but the atmosphere was light and serene. From my viewpoint on the street, I realized I was seeing my Grandma Boreman as a child.

Reflecting on both her age and the sidewalk in my dream made me think of her injury. In real life, she had tripped on an uneven sidewalk—hit her head so hard above her right eye that part of her skull became slightly sunken in. Through childhood and adolescence it stopped growing as fast as the rest of her head. She became incredibly self-conscious of the injury and styled her hair the same way to cover it. Her nose remained slightly crooked ever since.

Well, that's the story I recall. I'm not even sure who told me or when I first heard. *Did I make up that the damage was caused by a fall on a sidewalk?* Surely someone told me something similar for me to have assumed it's true. The older relatives might know.

I just didn't think they'd each have a different version of the story.

She fell on cement steps outside of their Akron home... No, she repeatedly ran into the corner of a table, and it did permanent damage to the right part of her head—it "cut off the blood vessel that controlled the growth section of her forehead"... She deliberately banged her head against the wall... Out of anger? Frustration? Sadness? *Wait.* Grandma banged her head against a wall *on purpose?*

But she was the oldest, they reminded me, and they were too little to remember what *actually* happened.

It seemed that Evelyn and her father were close, but I never got the sense she and her mother were or were not. After my question about the head injury, however, her brother (my great-uncle Harold) offered up more insight. "It was the beginning of the Depression and money [may] have been the reason they couldn't go to the hospital. She always had a grudge against her mom for not getting it treated. They weren't too close in their final years. Sad case."

But one thing I knew for certain about Grandma was her ability to use humor to bring levity—even under the most unfortunate and heartbreaking circumstances. And with that keen sense of humor, she would have the last laugh. No one could pull "an Evelyn" and take her picture—she had requested the casket stay closed at her funeral.

For a second, I thought about asking the funeral director to open the lid so I could snap a picture. "It's a family tradition," I'd say, explaining my odd request. But I chickened out. It wasn't fair.

She would be powerless to move out of the way, to cover her face, or choose to be the one behind the camera as she preferred to be. Instead, she would have to be seen.

PART II

CHAPTER 5

46% SCANDINAVIAN

Summer, 2015

Great News! Your AncestryDNA results are in!

For Father's Day I bought my dad a test kit. After only a few weeks and an email notification, answers to genetic mysteries have finally been bestowed upon us. Now to see where the elusive Lawrentz ancestors hailed from. The guesses our family held to were of English or Alsatian (from Alsace-Lorraine) descent.

It's been seven years since the Lawrentz homestead visit. During that time, I quit my first real grown-up job as a graphic designer to stay home with the two kids Jason and I brought into the world. I tried my hand at freelance design while I continued to chip away at our genealogy.

It's not a new pursuit. Family history has fascinated me since grade school. I would copy and draw my own family tree diagrams with the help and knowledge of my parents and grandparents. The dates I scrawled beside their names brought up visions of colonial silhouettes, spinning wheels, and folks churning butter. Watermen, farmers, and factory workers. I imagined what they looked like. If I had photos of them, I wondered if I could correctly gauge what personality traits they had based only on their expression. Which was consistently sour looking overall. If some future descendant of mine only had one picture of me in which to judge my personality, I don't think I'd like that very much.

My maternal grandfather, Harry "Stan" Scroggs, noticed my interest in genealogy and guided me to all kinds of resources. He had done family history research for decades—without the help of the internet. I made space for info sheets and binders from Grandpa on my bookshelf next to my personal journals and collection of Nancy Drews. I still have the handwritten note in red ink he placed as the first page in a binder he gave me when I was in sixth grade.

> *Dear Ali,*
>
> *I've put together a few family history things for you in a loose leaf. This will help you get started. I hope that this will be the beginning of many enjoyable hours, whether researching or just looking back on past family members and wondering how they lived and what it may have been like.*
>
> *There are many books in the libraries on beginning genealogy, so check them out and decide just how you want to go about it. I started back in the 1950's, sort of a trial and error thing, being self-taught, but I'd say do your own thing and set things up so that you understand and know how to interpret what info you have gathered.*
>
> *Good Luck, Grandpa Scroggs*

As he got older and I became more obsessed, we shared discoveries with one another, rather than just him sharing with me. Because they didn't have the internet, he relied on me and other family members to search for information online he couldn't find the old-fashioned way.

To keep hard copy records organized, you need office supplies. Lots. The man loved his office supplies, yet he would forget where he put them—then would inevitably buy more. After he died, I opened a cardboard box of his with "ALLISON" scrawled in permanent marker on one side. I peered in, curiously. It looked like he had robbed a Staples.

I would call him up, giddy with some small gem of information—a missing piece of something we'd been researching for a good length of time. It would fill me with pride to hear him so thrilled and chuckling that I had helped find the answer. I adored doing family history with him. And I adored him.

Online, I had millions of records (domestic and foreign) at my disposal, along with access to fellow researchers who could help provide additional information about the family. I couldn't help but feel a little guilty about the kind of access and resources I had without having to leave the house, while my grandfather had done all sorts of tedious work before. Regardless of how hard or easy the research was, the hunt was thrilling.

More answers brought more questions, and I lost track of time following the trail of clues down the rabbit hole of *Ancestry.com, FamilySearch. org,* and *Newspapers.com.* And now, I find myself right back in the thick of losing track of time with a new genealogy toy: the consumer DNA genetic test kits.

With my dad's test results waiting to be opened, I scrap the idea of waiting until he can view them with me—mostly since I have very little self-control when it comes to ignoring my own curiosity.

Click.

The first line I see shows a 46% Scandinavian estimate. Scandinavian? I haven't heard of any Nordic heritage before. Well, I have nothing to compare it to. His father may be Scandinavian for all I know. I guess I just figured that our hunch of thinking the Lawrentz family was Scotch-Irish, English, and/or Germanic would prove to be true.

Grandma's side would be German and Irish. Dad's Europe West region (which includes Germany, France, and Alsace) came in at 37% and Ireland only 7%. Great Britain looks to just be 3%. There are a couple other small percentages which are "low confidence" estimates. I thought he'd have way more German and Irish from both sides put together.

I should know better. I need to have an open mind about Phil's side— with the dreaded genealogical "brick wall" in my way throughout years of searching I really have no idea where the Lawrentz family came from. Even the distant cousins I've been connecting with for the last 11 years don't know for sure. If more of them start taking the DNA test, maybe we can make some progress in this area and can connect it back to some Scandinavian country.

My thoughts go to my fourth cousin, Robin Lawrentz (who was essential in helping piece together the Lawrentz family tree beyond Phil). Just a few months ago, he had suggested a link to Viking heritage through a branch of the Lawrentz family.

The Scandinavian percentage makes total sense then! No wonder my dad fits a stereotypical Viking description. I smirk, thinking of my 6' 2" red-headed, red-bearded father who my husband affectionately (and with a healthy fear of) calls "Big Mike." The same "Big Mike" he invited to lunch and asked for his blessing to have his oldest daughter's hand in marriage after dating her for only two months. Hence the healthy fear.

I notice a new feature on the DNA tests I'm an admin for. It's called "shared matches." Before this feature, you could see everyone's matches in a list (the other users who test and share DNA with you), but you couldn't see a list of matches only you yourself and another match had in common. But now with this new shared matches tool, it's going to open up a faster way to pinpoint who belongs to which side of the family.

Without much thought, I scroll intently through my dad's matches. Last names I know from Grandma's side jump out at me. England, Bowers, Prater, Gillespie...the list went on. Those were the Georgia relatives.

Grandma loved to remind me about her mother's family: The England relatives originally came from Ireland. There was always a satisfied snicker, as if you would never hear anything more amusing in your whole life.

I make little notes in the designated space and label them "Maternal side." Will dig into that later. Now, to find a few I can tell are from the paternal side so I can use the shared matches tool and really fill this tree out like a pro.

The first match has my attention. I notice the list is ordered from top to bottom with those who share the greatest amount of DNA at the top to the least amount at the bottom. Obviously, they must be someone pretty close in relation to Dad. Their Ancestry handle has "cbus" in the name and they match Dad at a "predicted 1st-2nd cousin" range. The "cbus" part has to mean they live in or are from Columbus. Only an hour from us.

I click on the name to view the shared matches. None of the ones I just marked being on Dad's maternal side. Okay! This means I have some paternal matches to work with now.

Online genealogy research always means messaging strangers, and many times you're messaging a stranger that's related to you. Albeit distantly, but related nonetheless. I wonder which crazy Lawrentz ancestor they are related to. Maybe I already know about them?

I start a new message.

"Hello! I did a DNA test for my dad, and it says that you may be 1st/2nd cousins—I was trying to figure out how that might be and if maybe we already know each other?"

I click *Send*.

I forget to follow up but after a month had passed I no longer need to; a message from them is waiting in my Ancestry inbox.

"What is your father's name? I don't recognize the last name. Is he from Ohio?"

Her name is Jennifer, she is around my age and (just as I suspected) lives near Columbus. We begin asking questions. A lot of questions.

"I am thinking that your dad is a second cousin...My mother's parents are from Mansfield, Ohio, with last names of Smith and Eckstrom." I tell her I'm at a loss on how to connect my dad to her. I've never heard of these names before that I could remember. *I'd remember, wouldn't I?*

We rapid fire more names and any bits we think would jog the other's memory to no avail.

A new thought lifts me out of my frustration: Here is a person my age, who lives only about an hour away, and we are both passionate about family history and genealogy like a couple of retired grannies. I smile as I glance back at our messages. 4:15 PM. 12:56 AM. 5:15 AM. 9:49 PM. 11:16 PM. I should be delighted she's just as interested in figuring out a new mystery with me as I am with her. I wonder if she's on the obsessive side like me. A stranger, but now family. Because the DNA tells me so.

I could bust through this Lawrentz brick wall for good if we can figure out our connection. I'm determined.

She asks for access to my private tree. I invite her several times over the course of the next year, but something is not working. Our messages slow to a crawl, and we don't get anywhere on the connection to my dad—and consequently the connection to each other.

❧

Summer, 2016

I wish Ancestry would just fix the problem. I nearly forgot all about it. Normally I would be in her shoes, once again reaching out to a distant cousin to remind them of whatever I had asked in the previous message. And here I am doing the same thing to Jen by forgetting or putting it off! She still hasn't been able to access my private tree for these last twelve months. I'm surprised I'm not more eager to get this technical glitch resolved.

The internal rant with myself is interrupted by something I hadn't considered. What if it's a sign to tread lightly? Or to not press into this Lawrentz connection at all. Maybe it *is* just best to leave it alone.

I let it go and let the summer fly by.

CHAPTER 6

INVESTIGATION

March, 2017

While I wait for this long winter to come to an end I focus my energy and time building out the Lawrentz tree. The goal is to discover more about Phil's siblings and where they ended up. I knew why we didn't know very much about my dad's paternal side. I knew enough not to ask too many questions. Dad's father, Phillip Earl Lawrentz, was estranged from the family. After the divorce, he had limited visitation rights which had to be supervised. By the time my dad and his younger brother Frank were teens, there was hardly any interaction with him. I was told the courts requested him to take a polygraph and go through a psychiatric examination in order to see the kids unsupervised and he refused.

When I would visit Grandma, I began using the time to ask her about Phil and where he came from. It was less about prying for information and learning about all of his misdeeds than it was about having this strong desire to learn about the Lawrentz heritage beyond him. I didn't know if I should even use his name—Phil—it almost felt like a bad word in our family. Usually he was referred to as "The Sperm Donor" or "The Creep." But Grandma was open to sharing and didn't seem disturbed or shut down by my questions, so I gently pressed on. I took notes. I learned a little more about just how dysfunctional things were and how Phil wasn't the only Lawrentz of his siblings with issues. I decided I could take comfort in knowing somewhat normal people came from this dysfunction. Somewhat.

With a new family history focus, I could continue to discover the rich history of the Lawrentz family before the chaos Phil and the instability his family branch brought to the tree. Surely there were redeeming stories and people to be proud of who lived before my dad's genetic father. I wanted to show my family the good. To give them something to be proud of.

A new message notification alerts me on Ancestry. It's from Jennifer: *Hi Allison, My Aunt Susie and her son, my first cousin Josh, recently took the test and are also a match to your dad.*

I feel a little embarrassed. Jen has tried to access my tree so many times over the last two and a half years, and it's never worked once. With not much faith that the issue would be solved, I send the link to my private tree once again.

And finally, for no apparent reason, it works.

With Jen's mom's sister Susie and her son Josh now in the database, we have enough DNA proof to show how Dad and Jen's connection stems from her mom's side of the family. I already knew the connection would link through the Lawrentzes. It's purely a process of elimination—either maternal or paternal. None of Grandma's relatives on his list showed up on Jen's. Or on Susie's or Josh's. I knew that even a hint of surnames like Bowers, England, or Prater within their matches would have indicated they were related to my grandma's side of the family. Dad's paternal relation it is.

Jen tells me about her maternal branch. Her grandfather, Leon Eckstrom, and her grandmother Wilma had seven daughters. Not one boy. Starting with Carol in the early 1940s, and ending with Karen at the end of the 1950s.

As a young man, Leon's father, Karl Ekström, sailed from Sweden to Ellis Island in 1914. He made his way to Chicago and then on to Davenport, Iowa, where he met and married Helen Magnus, a daughter of a Swedish

[ECKSTROM FAMILY TREE]

KARL Ekstrom — HELEN Magnus	JOHN Smith — IRENE Parks
CARL HELEN	DOROTHY WILLARD CARLTON ROBERT

LEON Eckstrom ———————————————— **WILMA** Smith

| CAROL | SYLVIA | LINDA | SUSIE | HELEN | DEBBIE | KAREN |

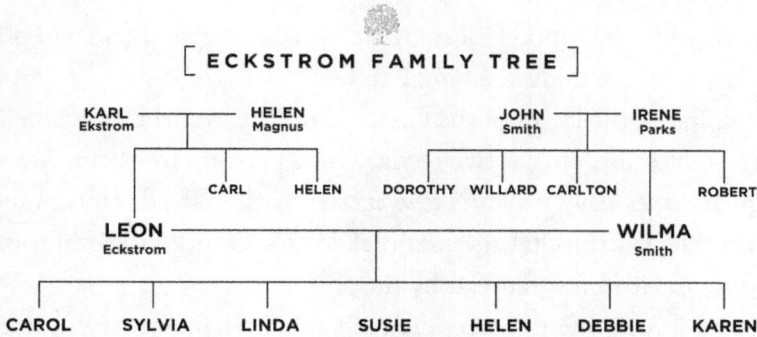

immigrant and a first generation Swedish-American.

When Leon and his younger brother Carl were around nine and eight years old, the family moved east to Mansfield, Ohio for work opportunities. A few years later in 1936, Karl and Helen would have a daughter.

Now armed with some foundational information from Jen, I can explore all kinds of records. I'm sure she is doing the same with all my Lawrentz info, but at this point what are we ultimately trying to find aside from the general *'how are we related'* question? I feel a little aimless in my investigating. How do we ultimately key in on the historic coordinates of our two families?

I scan through online articles from the *Mansfield News-Journal* for Leon's name and in no time, a few mentions of him catch my eye. In 1934, he was awarded a "Blue Star Writing Certificate" for penmanship from Prospect Elementary School.

Then in 1935, an article entitled "Shamar Wins" reads:

> *"... A puppy was offered to the boy who could suggest the best name for the sort of a dog used in the [motion] picture, and write the best 50-word letter telling why he selected that particular name. Leon suggested 'Shamar' and told why. He is 12 years old and a pupil at Hedge Street School."*

Next he appeared in a small article from 1937 describing an "instrumental number by Leon Eckstrom and Waldo Devore" at a women's church group held in the Main Street Evangelical Church with fifty members of their "Good Cheer Circle" in attendance. Leon had played the clarinet in the middle school band.

I can picture the ladies of the Cheer Circle sitting around white linen covered tables, listening as two teenage boys perform for them. A couple of regular Artie Shaws playing a few jazz standards of the day for contented rosy-cheeked matrons in hats and floral dresses. Or maybe they impressed the women with a few familiar hymns.

Jen and I continue to interview each other whenever new questions arise. I ask her how Leon and Wilma met. She sends me a picture of "the old man" and her grandma. They were high school sweethearts, attending Mansfield High together, just a year apart with Wilma graduating after Leon in 1941. They married in 1942. Shy and petite Wilma Smith was looking for a future that included a stable marriage and family with lots of love while Leon seemed to be hell-bent on getting his way at all costs.

Though he was an intelligent and enterprising businessman, most of Leon's behaviors were questionable. There was the cheating, the drinking, the stealing, the gambling. *"He could sell you something you already owned"* seemed to be the elevator pitch the family stuck with to introduce Leon to those who had never encountered him before.

I tell Jen some Phil stories and comment on how both of our grandmothers must have put up with so much. She agrees and we decide the two men are perfect for each other. Perhaps separated at birth.

Jen and I try to pinpoint a geographical location where our families may have crossed paths, but we also have to consider the timeline. Akron? They wouldn't have all been there at the same time. Leon *died* in Akron in 1999 and only lived there a short time near the end of his life, while Phil and Evelyn were both *born* in Akron but didn't stay as adults.

Leon and family lived in the Cleveland, Bucyrus, Mansfield, Galion, and Columbus areas. Bouncing from place to place and burning bridges, supposedly. But Jen and I kept coming back to Mansfield. It was the location the Eckstrom family spent the longest amount of time. With Ashland being a close neighboring town, Mansfield seemed a likely point of connection when compared to the others. Now I just need actual proof of any Eckstrom/Lawrentz paths crossing.

Phil worked for the Air National Guard at the Lahm Airport in Mansfield, which gave us our first Ashland-Mansfield connection. My family lived in Ashland while I grew up, but my dad worked for a bag company in Mansfield. We attended church in Mansfield, and it wasn't uncommon on weekends or weeknights for us to drive the 20-minutes south on Route 42 and go shopping at the Richland Mall and Value City Department Store for all the best deals on back to school clothes. And on special occasions, we'd head over to see the beautiful gardens at Kingwood Center and the peacocks that roamed its grounds. There were visits to the Richland Carousel where ornately hand-carved horses and menagerie of other colorful wooden animals raced around and around while rising and falling to the sound of calliope music—which I'm fairly sure played at an eardrum-bursting volume.

I start jotting down each piece of info I have on Phil's parents and siblings. How my dad and these three strangers (Jen, Susie, Josh) can be related just doesn't make any sense.

I edit down the list of possibilities to closer connections.

Could Phil be the father of both Susie *and* Jen's mom Helen? Seems far-fetched.

Maybe *he* is the one who isn't a Lawrentz? Now there's an idea worth exploring. *Could Phil be Leon's half-brother?* Dad could be a half-cousin to Susie and Helen.

Phil's mother Sylvia had eleven children that she claimed were *all* her husband Lida's children. I could only prove that six of the eleven could realistically be Lida's since he's recorded as deceased smack dab in the middle of Sylvia's pregnancy with baby #6. And since I am pretty sure we can rule out a birthing sextuplets scenario, it only leads me to ask who the father of the other five might be? I also can't realistically throw out the possibility of his mother having an affair while Lida was still living.

Sylvia did have a "wild streak," so said my grandma. She worked in a spaghetti house and loved to dance. Whatever your definition of wild is, I guess.

I recall an article from the *Akron Beacon* from 1921, reporting how Sylvia claimed her landlord attacked her. She then brought a lawsuit against him for $10,000 in damages. He claimed he was simply trying to collect the rent.

Only six years old when his father Lida died, Phil spent most of his young life in the County Home. His mother, struggling to take care of so many children, sent Phil and his younger brother Don away. Perhaps they were taken away, I don't really know. In and out of foster care for the rest of his childhood and teen years, Phil spent his senior year attending Ashland High School in 1946 and quickly became a Cadet for the Air National Guard.

The Phil/Leon being half-brothers hypothesis means we'd need proof that Karl "The Swede" Eckstrom got together with Sylvia Lawrentz around the fall of 1927.

Nope, that doesn't add up. Karl and Helen were still living in Davenport, Iowa, with their young two sons in 1927, while Sylvia was in Akron, perhaps hoping to still collect that $10K from her landlord.

Okay, what about this:

Phil was said to have bragged about his "conquests" to his brothers-in-law and to friends. Gross. I remember learning about his time in Mansfield at the Lahm Military Airport. With the National Guard and stationed in Germany in the early 1950's. Maybe *he* had other children we didn't know about. Kids in Germany? Kids in Mansfield? Both?

I ponder over stories I had been told throughout the years. Without telling her parents, the recently engaged Evelyn went to Reverend Clymer's two-story yellow house on Maple Street to have the middle-aged preacher marry her and Phil. Mae and her new husband Art "stood up for them" just like Phil and Evelyn had for them at the reverend's place only a couple months before.

When Grandma recalled the moment to me she added, "[Phil] asked—after we got married—he says, 'Now what if I don't want to be married?' The preacher says, 'Well, you'll have to go to the courthouse, that's not in my line of work.'" I asked if that bothered her. "Oh, I didn't care," she said dismissively.

Together with their only witnesses, Art and Mae, the four set off to Mansfield for dinner and a movie. *So Dear to My Heart* with Burl Ives, this time. Mae and Art's after-ceremony motion-picture had been *Paleface* with Bob Hope and Jane Russell.

When the new Mrs. Phillip Lawrentz got home, she told her parents the news. "My mother went upstairs and cried," she recalled.

Soon, the family grew to like Phil: he had a good job, was friendly enough, and their "LaRue" would be taken care of. A little girl, Linda Louise, was born in August of 1950 to Evelyn and Phil. By 1953 the little family lived in a duplex on Miller Street across from the YMCA. The couple that occupied the other half of the duplex? Mae and Art. "There was a door connecting the two residences on the inside," Mae had shared with me. "It was never shut. [Evelyn and I] were always together."

Around 1954, they both moved to different homes in the Ashland community. After a very short time on Garfield Avenue and a new addition to their family that December (baby Jimmy), they moved to nearby East Walnut Street in November of 1955.

As their families grew, Evelyn and Mae remained friends. Their kids played together, and since Grandma was a full-time homemaker, she often babysat Mae's children while her friend continued to pursue a career.

On December 18, 1959, almost five years after Jim was born, the Lawrentzes welcomed another son, my dad Phillip Michael Lawrentz. Frank, their third son arrived just shy of three years after Mike. And so, like a carbon copy of the Frank and Grace Bowers family, Phil and Evelyn's family consisted of one girl followed by three boys.

A few months after Frank's birth in 1962, they moved out of the Walnut Street house and out of Ashland. They found a newer construction house for sale, a modern ranch, in the small town of Shelby just north of Mansfield. This move would allow Phil to be closer to his new job with Friebel and Hartman as a purchasing agent.

But the stay at the new home wouldn't last long. While Phil remained at his job, the family of six moved back to Ashland in less than two years.

This time they found a house on East Washington Street, just a block over from their old Walnut Street neighborhood.

Soon, things had completely unraveled, Evelyn and Phil separated and divorced by late spring of 1966. After hearing stories of abuse and the trauma he inflicted, I always wondered why it took her seventeen years to file for divorce.

I never met Phil. I was told the closest I came to "meeting" him was when he showed up on our front porch when I was a baby. Mom and I stayed inside while Dad stepped out the front door to talk to his estranged father, refusing to let him in.

While Leon relied on alcohol (so much so he kept a flask of whisky under the driver's seat of his car), Phil was a teetotaler. It was their abusive nature that seemed to be the commonality between the two men.

Jen asks me in a new message, "When did Phil and Evelyn get married?" I answer.

She must be working on her suspicions, too. I wonder what they are.

I ask, "When did Leon and Wilma divorce?" She answers.

We both ask each other, "Did your grandma work out of the home?"

And on and on we curious sleuths inquire.

The end of March is here.

Truths hidden in piles of research and conversation begin their whispering. Maybe I know it subconsciously. But that *can't* be right and I'm sorry for even considering it. There is *zero* sense in this possibility.

There's a logical explanation, I'm sure! An obvious one! A scientific one, even! If I just exclaim it enough with exclamations it will be so!

So, for just a second, I entertain the whispers rising to the surface from their deep hiding places. Because what *if?* One whisper is a little louder than the others and I am left with nothing else to do but listen.

CHAPTER 7

TOP OF THE WORLD
Spring, 2006

*E*ngaged to be married, starting a full-time design job and finishing my last semester of college proved quite enough for me to handle all at one time.

I had been working on a series of mixed-media paintings for our senior exhibit opening right before graduation. I titled the pieces: *From Year to Year, Shut Down, Silenced, Healing,* and *Herstory.*

From Year to Year took up the entire width of a small wall to the right of the exhibit's entrance. It was a collage of women's faces, torn pieces of sheet music, even a lock of my own hair, since I'm dramatic like that. Placed throughout the work were lithographs I had done reminiscent of Nancy Drew using a magnifying glass as well as some extra copies of old black and white family pictures. I glued, printed, painted, drew, and splashed beeswax over all of it.

Installed above the piece was a small wooden shelf which held a few old puzzle pieces on its ledge. These pieces were all from one puzzle (a scene of a non-Disney version of Peter Pan's *Neverland)* and they were not in great shape; most of the original pieces had been missing from the canister for as long as I can remember.

I felt the need to understand my grandma's life beyond the stories and photos I grew up knowing. Making art was a way I could process through that curiosity. Maybe it was stubborness or obsessiveness but I couldn't help but wonder about all the things she didn't speak about. It was heartbreaking to think she had stopped dreaming about finding the perfect life she may have envisioned as a young woman. Her dreams had now become unattainable, lost, taken, or beaten out of her in one form or another.

Her unrealized and mostly unverbalized hopes and dreams were replaced with the large and small traumas that dotted her life. The expectations, suppression, and unbalanced submission I saw in even the seemingly "happy" lives of women in my family seem to chase after them generation after generation. I didn't want that to happen to me.

I had come too close to a relational dumpster fire before. Completely enthralled by someone intense and deep, brooding, complicated... I seemed to think I could round out his rough edges. He could be charming and romantic but under all the charisma and eloquent words hid narcissism, gaslighting, manipulation, and a brewing violence. I don't even think he understood it. The idea that a dark generational stronghold I had no real knowledge of as a naïve teenager could have manifested in some shadow-like parallel life haunted me. History could very well have repeated itself because of my innocent ignorance and immaturity.

I'm thankful I lost my footing on that possible life path through no decision of my own. He broke up with me. Reeled me back in for a blip of time, unsure if he really wanted it to be over, but then ultimately let me go again. Maybe he loved me enough to let me go. Or maybe he knew I'd never be what he wanted me to be. My inexperienced heart suffered and grieved for longer than I care to admit. Either way, I eventually matured enough to understand it as a gift of protection, and a renewed vision of God's plan for my life.

When I observed Grandma, I saw a woman who put herself aside for her loved ones and friends. I think she preferred that over focusing on her own needs. She didn't want to be the center of attention or anywhere close. She'd never want to "bother" anyone. Hearing the negative things she'd say about herself made me sad because I knew she didn't see herself like we did.

Sometimes she'd get her picture taken with family or friends—always a slightly closed-lipped smile—while other times I'd see her sticking a hand up in front of her face when a camera appeared. She loved taking pictures, just not being in them.

But why the interest in photography? Maybe it was the art of it, the hobby. Perhaps it was one of the few things she had control over in her life. She could choose when she had the camera in hand. She could control a piece of the narrative behind the camera. Or maybe, if she was the one with the camera it could always get her out of being in the photo. I started looking at her photos in a new way. Instead of dwelling on the subjects in the picture, it made me think about her. *Click. Wind. Click. Wind.*

Behind the scenes, she was getting to make a choice of what moment she wanted to capture. What she wanted to remember and what she wanted to keep.

In *Shutdown,* I painted a woman emotionally paralyzed. Buried in so much heaviness the only way to survive was to shut down. If you don't stir up trouble, you don't get noticed. You learn how to survive in that reality after a while, but lose yourself in the process.

In *Silenced,* I painted a woman underwater. A hand, palm out to the viewer trying to reach out and connect. But no one would be able to hear her down there. It's peaceful, floating in blues and greens, and her long hair flows around her. Freedom and hope are present, but if she could just make it out of the deep waters of losing her voice, she had so much to offer the world.

Healing was a bit more optimistic. With a woman half in shadow and half in light, she seemed to be emerging out of the chaos and the pain of her life. Strong enough to move forward into her story. The story she wanted to tell.

My final piece of the series was *Herstory.* I painted the profile of my grandma from a 1940s photograph, holding a few kittens in a garden and sporting a cute wavy bob haircut. I left out the kittens and the short hair and instead gave her long, colorful, flowing locks which took up almost the entire canvas. In the left mid-section of the painting there was room for a grid-like element. It contained other female faces. Other women from my family. Some were well kept inside those boxes. Others were starting to emerge.

But she—she had gotten out. She was larger than life and free. I wanted it to be my grandma's story. I think she had wanted it to be her story, too. A life where her thoughts and feelings weren't dismissed. One where her diaries weren't gathered up and thrown into a fire. One where she wasn't called names. One where she was asked what she thought. One where she didn't have to wonder if the men she chose to love would treat her and her children with kindness, gentleness, and respect.

The version of her in my painting would be a woman who felt free to tell her whole story and not be burdened with secrets and shame.

I created those pieces for my grandma and the other women in my family who had no voice at one time or another. And for their children who would grow up already having lost some of their voice at a very young age.

In the midst of working on that series, I had stumbled upon the song "Top of the World" by Patty Griffin. The way it symbolically presented the emotionally and verbally wounded person in the song to a bird, struck a dissonant chord in me. I felt like it could have swallowed me whole. The once detached observer sings how they realize they had been the cause of the bird's song being suppressed and finally silenced. They were filled with remorse for what could have been. But it was too late.

Where there was once hope and excitement for what the future held, the fledgling no longer resembled itself. There still may have been feathers on the fragile bird, but with broken wings there is no chance for it to fly or sing again.

Each time I played "Top of the World" it was as if I could substitute the songbird for several crushed spirits throughout our family tree. Mostly, I thought of Grandma and cried extra tears she couldn't.

The men who caused much of this pain had lost their true selves—who they were really supposed to be. Once they were just little boys with dreams. With tender hearts and mommies. I decided the paintings were about them, too.

I had learned bits of their stories. Their own trauma as children, mental illnesses left untreated, emotional needs unmet. They were then left to deal with their pain on their own. A society which said women were secondary to men; weaker and less intelligent. A society which said it wasn't okay to get help. Just be a man. But in trying to be men, they ended up facing their demons alone—and the demons took over. They became prisoners of pride and power, greed and lust. What if they were doing the best they could? Or would that be letting them off too easy?

What if they wanted to know others, and they wanted to be known back? They were hurt, and instead of heading for the light, they buried themselves in a dark place and lost their identity in the process. What could a person forgive? What would they ultimately be remembered for?

She came with my parents and a few family friends to see the exhibit that spring. I was too timid to tell Grandma how much she inspired those paintings, but I pointed out places where I used her likeness. With her bright blue windbreaker and sheer floral scarf around her head, she agreed to pose for a few pictures with me and the paintings *Silenced* and *Herstory*. An old lady now, but still standing.

On one visit to her house, Grandma surprised me with an envelope. "Don't show your dad," she said. I opened it to find two photos. The first showed an older man in a plain white T-shirt with large bifocals and a long scraggly beard, thinning hair on the very top, staring right at the camera like he was in a lineup. The other photo was the back side of him, showing off how long the hair on his head had gotten—or what was left of it. "10 months growth" was written on the back of the image. The old man was Phil. I wasn't sure why she thought to show it to me.

"His wife Helen sent me that."

"Why?" I asked, trying not to sound too disgusted. "Did you ever tell her what he did?" I asked like I had been there and knew all he had done.

"No, she asked me why his kids never wanted to see him all this time. I wouldn't want to talk bad about him to her."

I didn't understand.

CHAPTER 8

THROUGH THE LOOKING GLASS
April, 2017

*S*pring decides to finally make an appearance, but it's Ohio and I don't expect it to stay. At least it's warm enough for sitting on the front porch with my coffee. I settle myself into the cheap, plastic Adirondack chair and remember a time not long ago when I'd have to pop up at a moment's notice and save Miles' blankie from his little sister's clutches. Or save Clementine's binkie from the filthy porch floor.

My wind chime gives a voice to the light breeze. With both kids now in school, instead of watching my own brood I watch the robins hop in our postage stamp corner lot to find food for their babies.

The mourning doves are back. They like to nest in the same protected corner of the porch where the brick column meets the white and chipping bead-board ceiling that ought to be painted a pale robin's egg blue.

Freelance is slow, and I don't mind. It's mid-morning, and every so often, a car drives too fast down Eastern Avenue, but I'm used to the rhythm and the noise. I hum along with the song playing out of my phone's speaker, glad for the rhododendrons, mature and mangled, that bookend and wrap around my porch with their glossy thick leaves and twisted, sprawling branches. They give me just the right amount of privacy and false sense of security I need on my corner lot porch.

Last sip of coffee.

I get up from my chair and head inside. Time to open the laptop and scroll through Facebook, look at emails (if there are any), and of course check to see if I have any new Ancestry messages.

On certain days, like today, the kitchen counter doubles as my desk. After a few clicks, I see a message waiting for me on Ancestry. It's from Jen.

"Can you click the '*i*' button on your dad and my Aunt Susie's matches page to see the shared DNA centimorgans? I share 780cMs with your dad!"

My eyes squint to focus on the '*i*'. Where did that come from? Why hadn't I seen it before? My fingers start typing a response. "I didn't know you could do that! He shares 1,740cMs with your aunt, and 868cMs with your cousin Josh!" Using exclamation points as if I know what I am talking about or confident of what those numbers could possibly mean.

Jen is floored. I want to be floored! What am I missing here? She must see the dots in the message box tapping out their steady beat as I type. I pause. I type some more and erase it. Finally, I stick with, "What do you think that means?" I decide I want her thoughts first.

While I wait for her take on things, I hunt down a chart about centimorgans (cMs). I find a simple chart which helps determine relationships between people based on how many cMs they share with each other.

- A full child/parent or identical twin will be right around 3,400cMs
- A full sibling will have somewhere between 2,400-2,800cMs
- A first cousin: a range of 680-1,150cMs
- A grandparent, aunt/uncle, niece/nephew, or half-sibling should have 1,320-1,700cMs

The chart points me to what possible relationships Jen's Aunt Susie and my dad have with their 1,740cMs of shared DNA. There are a few to pick from. A weird version of choose your own adventure. Grandparent, aunt/nephew, uncle/niece, or half-sibling. I squint harder. Grandparent? Doubtful. Aunt/nephew or uncle/niece? Reasonable. I can't rule it out because of a situation like this on my mom's side where my grandma is close in age to her mother's younger siblings.

Jen's three dots stop and her message pops up on my screen. "Well... the charts I am looking at show that 1,740 would put Susie and your dad right at the average cm match for a half-sibling, or an aunt/uncle, niece/nephew relationship. Given the close ages, half-sibling to my mom and her sisters? That would be crazy! Maybe way off for me to suggest! BUT the range for half uncle is 540-1348, average of 892, which would match where Josh and I fall in relation with your dad as well... I've been meaning to also tell you that Leon had red hair. I noticed some gorgeous red hair in your family. Aunt Susie is also a natural redhead."

I relax my face only because it hurts to keep it scrunched up. But the sinking feeling in my stomach persists. On the other hand, there is a rush of anticipation and excitement that drives my need to know more.

She continues and reminds me of the birth order of the sisters. The youngest, Karen, she types, was born in December of 1959. I recall an earlier conversation with Jen when she had mentioned that Karen was the same age as my dad. I cross my eyes at the thought of what all of it means and decide I'll unpack that tangled mess later. I try not to let the old and new information muddle my newfound focus of proving my hypothesis that Phil had fathered other children. I had names and DNA proof: Susie and Helen. A good genealogist would test their own hypothesis to disprove it. If I can't disprove it, then it means it's possible.

I know just the thing to check. Robin Lawrentz' name will show up on Dad's DNA match list and it will show a third cousin centimorgan range. Then I can ask Jen to consider that her grandmother may have had at least her mom Helen and her Aunt Susie with my grandfather Phil. I can show her the facts and be patient as she processes the truth of how we're related. Having new family members we didn't know existed is actually extremely exciting! I wonder if they have similar mannerisms. What were their lives like growing up? There's so much catching up to do.

I find Robin's username. *Click.* "roblawrentz is not on your DNA match list" with the disclaimer: "This person is either not a DNA match or has not taken a DNA test." Okay—he probably hasn't taken it yet. Maybe I can see if he'd be willing to do the test soon to help make things clear for Jen and her family. I type out a quick message to Robin and hit send.

More waiting, but it'll be worth it.

It's evening and the magnetic grip of curiosity yanks me back to my computer. Jason is reading and the kids are finally asleep. Or at least in bed, which is still a win. Bottom line: it's quiet enough to do some digging.

Bringing up a yearbook search on *Ancestry.com*, I type in *Eckstrom* and *Ohio* in the search fields. Two names I recognize appear in the search results. Carol and Sylvia. The oldest daughters of Leon and Wilma. I click on Sylvia's name from the 1960 Madison High School yearbook in Mansfield. A full-page scanned image appears. Glancing down the list of student names on the freshman page I quickly find *Eckstrom*. Sylvia in the fifth row, second from the left. I stare at the black and white image of a young girl with short wavy hair and glasses, posed looking away from the camera. There's a smile on her face but I can't tell if it's an honest-to-goodness true one or not. Whatever kind of smile it was, it shows a slight gap in her front teeth. I've seen this face before.

I click on the blue *Ps* square in the dock of my MacBook and Photoshop bounces open. I also open my half-way organized/half-way wreck of a family photos digital folder. There. *That one.* It was not from Dad's freshman year of high school; in fact, he was much younger in this school photo, maybe third or fourth grade. But it was the same angled pose. Same wavy hair, just shorter. Glasses. Partially open smile. Gap. I layer the image of my dad next to the one of Sylvia and stare.

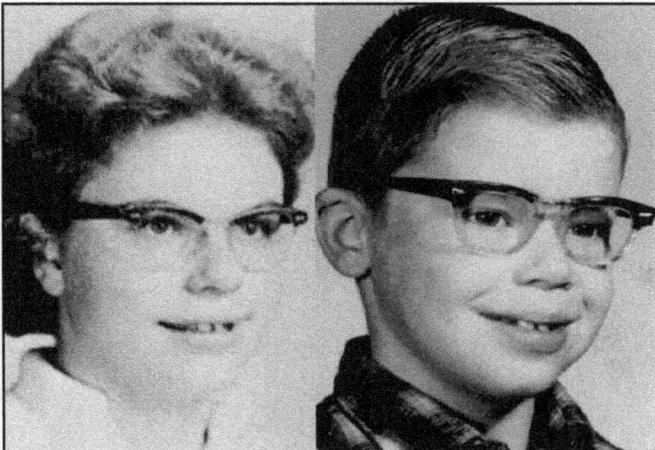

Sylvia, 1960   Mike, 1967

Each Saturday morning we do family breakfast at my parents' house. While I love these family times together, there is less time to obsess over yearbooks, census records, and city directories. Maybe I'll bring my computer in case I have time to scroll. But first, a more important matter: my mom's breakfast smorgasbord.

We drive across town and arrive last, but they've waited for us. After blessing the food, we dig in. There's a frenzy of activity in addition to the whole eating part. A mix of bluegrass, newgrass, and country-rock tunes come through the speakers rigged into the dining room from my dad's six-disc CD player in the rec room. A dial on the wall at about the second carpeted step down to the finished basement allows us to turn the volume of the Eagles or The Nitty Gritty Dirt Band up or down.

I eat entirely too much then grab my computer and open it right at the table. But my sharing impulse is kicking in. *Don't talk about Jen and the details; you're just doing a quick show and tell with the Sylvia yearbook photo.* I shouldn't show until I know more... but I can't help myself.

Turning the laptop screen to show my mom and sisters, Dad asks me, "Where did you find this?" I realize I may have offered too much too soon. My answer squeaks out like a question and without any sarcasm. "The internet?" I might as well have accusingly pointed my finger at the computer screen; like a scared child blaming the family dog for breaking some valuable heirloom. *I didn't do it! It was the internet!*

Back home we continue our normal Saturday afternoon. Everyone is occupied in the living room, TV on, toys tossed all around. I pull the charging cord from my laptop and casually find my spot on the couch and quietly hinge it back open. Maybe no one will notice. I glance over at Jason in his recliner to find him staring at me. Well, that was short lived. He smiles. I say nothing to defend myself and bury my attention in records. When will I learn enough to be satisfied?

I should look up Leon in the yearbook search catalog next, just for kicks. I find a full class photo from his Junior year at Mansfield Senior High School and one from his Senior year in 1940. He's wearing a thin jacket over a striped shirt and styling some very slicked back hair. I study his face. Was that a cigarette or a pencil behind his ear? Looks like he's part of the T-Birds gang from an early version of *Grease* or something.

I remember Jen and I had exchanged some family photos and I locate the one she sent me of the Eckstrom sisters taken in recent years. I study this new picture as well, memorizing names to faces. I snap myself out of the facial feature analysis trance. It's time to take some research risks.

I think about Aunt Linda. She suffered from ovarian cancer and had gone into remission for a while, but it came back. I wish she were here because I wish she wasn't gone, but I also wish she was here because I get the feeling she could have answers to most of my questions. The thought of it makes me feel guilty.

Strategy mode. I can ask my uncles. Would they even go for it? If they do agree to take a DNA test, at least it will be a convenient undertaking. They all work together at Dad's packaging business.

I begin a new email.

"Question for you, as I continue my family history research: Would either of you be interested in doing the Ancestry DNA like Dad did? It would be interesting to see how yours all compare... Putting some missing pieces together for our Scandinavian roots! Or at least *Dad's* test came back with a whopping 46% Scandinavian! So, I was curious if you all had as high of a percentage as well. Might show us some new cousins or close relatives. Having a few matches show up in Dad's that I'm trying to see how they are connected. Having additional testers from the same family helps confirm. If you are interested let me know. No pressure, but thought I'd run it by you." *Send.*

A couple days pass by. I get replies from them both.

I'm relieved. They agree to test.

It may stir up more questions than answers, but finding out their DNA origin estimate, shared matches, and cMs with each other will be the additional information I need to prove—whatever it is I need to prove.

What I need to do now is make a timeline.

While I'm waiting for an Ancestry sale, I might as well go full-on crazy, red-string thumb-tack sleuth. I type up every date and fact I have collected on Leon G. Eckstrom and Phillip E. Lawrentz from the time they were born until their death.

※

Getting ready for bed, I stand at the bathroom sink and grab my contacts case. I hesitate before peeling one of the lenses out of my eye. While I can still see clearly, I sit the case back down on the countertop and stare hard at my own face in the mirror. There's an element of both vanity and judgment in the act of looking at your own image. But this time isn't about determining whether I have a good face or a bad face or which feature is ugly or pretty. I'm looking for clues and answers.

Focusing on the shape of my face, my red hair, freckles, and a nose which I've never settled on whether it was from one side of the family or the other I think about all of the Eckstrom photos I had seen over the last few weeks. I can't deny there is something familiar about their faces I'm seeing in my own.

CHAPTER 9

THE TRUTH OF THESE MATTERS
April, 2017

"The act of recording the present is the key to remembering the past."
(A line from Grandma's 1940s high school diary cover page.)

I find a couple of open parking spots and pull into the nearest one. Grabbing my purse, I make sure I have my keys, phone, and wallet, hop out of the minivan, and slam the door shut. I press the lock button a bunch of times—just to be sure—and dart up the sandstone steps. I only have an hour, tops. No one is in sight as I let myself in and make my way around unmanned metal detectors. I rehearse my answer to the question, "What can I help you find?" as I climb up the shiny marble staircase to the Clerk of Courts office. I hope I can focus and not get distracted with other records I could pull.

I open the clerk's heavy wooden door. The woman across the counter is a classmate of my dad's. She seems to recognize me, too.

"Hi there! You are Mike's daughter, right?"

"Hello, yes that's me!"

"Oh, the pictures I see of your kids on your dad's Facebook wall are so cute. They are really growing up!"

I thank her and smile and think she probably remembers my face but not my name. "Yes, it goes so fast!" When the opportunity presents itself, I try to respond in cliches before the other person does. I don't give her time to serve any small talk back to me, and I get down to business.

"I'm trying to find a divorce record...um...it would be for 1966, I think..." I *think?* Why am I playing dumb? As if I was just in the neighborhood, so I thought I'd stop by and look up my grandparents' divorce record for fun?

Feeling the need to explain more, I add, "My dad's parents split up when he was really little, you know; he went from Lawrentz to his step-dad's last name, Boreman, then back to Lawrentz...I'm just curious what the file would say about it—I'm sort of the family historian of the bunch..."

If I did one thing well, it was giving unneeded details in hopes of convincing people I had valid reasons for whatever I was up to. She's nodding along with my run on sentence as I trail off. Over-explaining tends to run in the family.

"Oh, sure! Well, you're gonna want to look at these large books right over here...the names are listed like this...and when you find the corresponding number let me know and I'll help you find the microfilm roll it's on..." Her willingness to help eases my anxiety about what I might find. I still feel a bit like a private investigator, but mostly like a naughty child, digging for information on dead relatives without permission.

Carefully scanning the yellowed pages in the giant book full of names and numbers, I hurry myself along, though no one is rushing me.

There. Lawrentz....Bowers...Phillip Lawrentz and Evelyn Bowers. Case number 208.

I get my friend the clerk's attention and she gets me set up on the microfilm machine. Microfilm? Microfiche? *Microfiber?* No, that's not right. I make a mental note not to say any of them to her.

I hadn't been on one since I was in middle school at the public library reference room. Endlessly curious, I looked up newspaper articles about the "haunted" Riddle Schoolhouse located near my friend's country home.

We had ventured out into her woods to find it one day. That was after we hunted for arrowheads and crayfish in the shallow creek and came upon a deep pink colored hummingbird, perfectly still and stiff on the ground. We made Fuchsia a little grave under a tree in her yard.

So many things have still yet to be digitized, even with the millions of records accessible online. Since Ashland is a small town, most things (I assume) will have to be approached the "old-fashioned" way. I take a seat.

The machines are dinosaurs. Which is fitting because it even sounds like a velociraptor when I zoom too far one way or the other. She tells me if I see a page I want to print, just click the green button. Copies are 5 cents each.

I thank her and she leaves me to my search. "It's a small file," she had said about case number 208, but I start wondering how large the average file is. For a "small" one, it seems to have quite a few pages to skim through.

I'm tempted to read each line, but instead I press the green button as many times as there are pages to look them over at home. There I won't feel rushed. The paper is still warm in my hands as I grab my purse from beside me on the floor and head to the main desk. Placing my printouts on the counter, she counts them out while I count my change. I smile, thanking her and leave my 35 cents on the counter.

With the copies tucked in my arm and held to my chest, I wheel out the door, glide down the marble steps past the metal detector (still unmanned) and out the front doors. Popping my sunglasses on my face, I imagine I just got away with something.

At home, I get comfortable on the couch, photocopies in hand. The pages have long cooled off but my hands and face both feel hot.

The first page I read is the Petition for Divorce from May 6, 1966. Happy belated birthday, Phil.

"Evelyn L Lawrentz, Plaintiff vs. Phillip Lawrentz, Defendant.

She and the Defendant were married at Ashland, Ohio, on February 12th, 1949. Four children being born of said marriage. To wit: Linda Louise, age 16 years; James Russell, age 12 years; Phillip Michael, age 6 years; and Frank Robert, 3 years. That the parties have been living separate and apart since March 28, 1966. That the Defendant has been guilty of extreme cruelty towards Plaintiff and that he has carried on a constant and continuous course of wrongful conduct towards Plaintiff, which conduct has seriously affected the physical and mental well-being of Plaintiff, making it impossible for the parties to continue to live and co-habit together as man and wife."

Towards *Plaintiff.* It's odd to me how it doesn't mention any physical or mental distress caused to the children, just to Grandma.

Twenty days after the Petition for Divorce was dated, a restraining order was filed. I wonder if this was before or after Phil stole some of her photos. I remember Dad telling me what a big deal it was to her and how, when he was older, he mustered up the courage to go to Phil's house and get most of them back for his mom.

"Now comes the Plaintiff and says that the Defendant herein has been for the past two and one-half weeks annoying her by constant harassment in that he has entered upon the home premises of the parties occupied by the Plaintiff at any and all hours of the night causing disturbance in the Plaintiff's household and depriving the Plaintiff and the children of the parties of their rest and peace of mind. Wherefore, Plaintiff moves the Court for a temporary restraining order enjoining Defendant from molesting, annoying, or interfering with the Plaintiff and/or the minor children of the parties in any manner whatsoever during the pendency of this suit, and further enjoining Defendant from entering upon the home premises of the parties now occupied by the Plaintiff during the pendency of this action."

Since there were children involved, someone had to come and make sure the home was satisfactory to live in. A divorce investigator named Judith A. Burns and a domestic relations officer, Charles F. Adams, signed this document from June 21st.

It states:

"Plaintiff and four children are residing in the home of the parties at 211 East Washington Street, Ashland, Ohio. The home was found to be clean and in a neat and orderly condition. The two-story house has four bedrooms and provides adequate space for the children. The

children of the parties would appear to be healthy and well cared for. Linda, aged 16, apparently helps her mother quite a bit with the younger children and the housework. At this time, the Plaintiff has not settled employment outside the home. She does some part-time work as a demonstrator for Tri-Chem paint products. The Plaintiff stated that if the divorce is granted, she will have to find employment outside of the home. She is to receive $40 per week support from the Defendant and it will be necessary for her to go to work... The monthly expenses for this household would run at least $250. The Plaintiff's parents are Mr. and Mrs. Frank Bower[s] of 924 Lee Avenue, Ashland, Ohio. The children of these parties would appear to have a very negative attitude toward their father which appeared to me might have been caused by their mother's comments against him."

"Caused by their mother's comments..." Listen Judith, how about you keep your assumptions to yourself and just report the facts.

"The Defendant is presently residing at 304 College Avenue, Ashland, Ohio. He is employed at the Mansfield Airport and the Plaintiff states that he has a net pay of approximately $428 per month. The Defendant is also a member of the Air National Guard. The Defendant's father is deceased and his mother is Mrs. Sylvia Lawrentz of Akron, but the Defendant and his 11 brothers and sisters were raised in a county home in Akron."

What wasn't Grandma telling the authorities? No doubt she withheld information that could call for more serious action against Phil. Was she protecting him? Or was she protecting herself and the kids?

Another motion was filed but then dismissed by July 28th. It read:

"Now comes the Plaintiff and moves the court for a new trial or rehearing on the following grounds. 1.) Irregularity in the proceedings of the court in taking judicial notice of a former divorce proceeding between different parties in the same court. 2.) Error in the proceedings of the court in considering evidence obtained through means outside

of the evidence such as telephone calls to the court's office, whereby Plaintiff was prevented from cross-examination of possible witnesses. 3.) Court committed prejudicial error in considering matters from its own knowledge 4.) The court erred in considering the doctrines of recrimination and can condonation neither being plead.

Silverling & Anderson, Attorneys"

The memo at the bottom states:

"The court will recall that immediately prior to hearing the evidence in this cause a case entitled 'Boreman' was held by the court in which certain testimony relating to the Plaintiff was adduced. This case went forward immediately and no opportunity was given this Plaintiff in this court to either be aware of or prepared to offer any contra testimony. After trial and before the Court's judgment was rendered on July 1, 1966, counsel for Plaintiff learned that the Court secretary had received a phone call from a neighbor pertaining to both the Boreman and the Plaintiff's case. Whether this information received over the phone was relayed to the Court is unknown to the Plaintiff; however, Plaintiff feels, that in all fairness, she should be given an opportunity to subpoena such a neighbor such as Mr. Boreman and Mrs. Boreman and others to get at the truth of these matters in open Court...

The pertinent case to support Plaintiff's motion is the case of Opperman vs. Opperman... *This case holds that it is prejudicial for a court to take judicial notice of former divorce proceedings between different parties in the same court or in considering matters from its own knowledge. This case factually was one that the Plaintiff during a separation from her husband kept company with a man who had secured a divorce in the same court while he was so keeping company..."*

The Mr. Boreman mentioned, of course, is our future Grandpa Boreman. Growing up, it never dawned on me she and Phil had divorced the same year she and Grandpa got married. There was extremely little time in between the relationships. In fact, it sounded like Grandma was seeing ol' Petermo while the proceedings with Phil were still happening. And

Pete's own divorce wasn't final either. No wonder they drove down to Winchester that October to get married—who would want to go back to the same courthouse you both just got divorced in? Not to mention the small-town gossip mill.

Apparently, there was already one nosey neighbor calling in to tattle on the 38-year-old Evelyn. Aside from the Gladys Kravitz copycat I'm just learning about, I recall a story I was told years ago about her pastor showing up at the doorstep to make it explicitly clear that Evelyn understood divorce was a sin. Helpful.

Even at a young age, I remember us kids having a general understanding of Grandpa Boreman being our step-grandpa and how he was married before. Never was it kept secret from us. There was nothing to hide. We were given the story that his first wife was "the town floozy" and he just wouldn't tolerate it. So, he got a divorce. A bit scandalous to my school-age mind, but simple enough to understand. Yet, in their petition for divorce, I discovered it was *his wife* who filed, not Grandpa.

Margaret Boreman, Plaintiff vs. Donald Boreman, Defendant: For reasons of *"gross neglect of duty and extreme cruelty"* Again with the extreme cruelty.

The petition was filed May 9, 1966, only *three days* after Grandma's petition. By July 9th, the divorce was granted.

As for Evelyn and Phil's ongoing case, fast-forward to March of 1967. It seemed that Phil had filed a motion against her for not allowing visitation once a week and that she was failing to pay the children's hospitalization insurance as the divorce agreement had stated. Grandma's reasoning was since Phil had not been sending child support payments (even though he was making enough money) she couldn't afford to pay on insurance—it was hard enough to keep her kids fed.

My guess is Grandpa Boreman found it difficult to stomach Phil coming around once a week to visit the kids or it had become more evident to Grandma that her kids were in danger being around their father. I imagine Phil saying something like: *Fine. I'll stop sending you money.* Well, things backfired on Phil, and Grandma was not held in contempt of the court.

The divorce agreement was amended, and (for the most part) in her favor. *"...[It is necessary for the court to make the following order] for the welfare of the children..."*
Regarding child support and insurance:

"...Beginning March 7th in 1967, the plaintiff [this time, Phil] shall pay to the defendant the sum of $190 per month applicable to the support of the minor children of the parties...the plaintiff shall [pay for insurance for the children,] for uninsured medical optical and dental bills for the children...that exceeds $50 per child."

Visitation rights? He no longer has time alone with them:

"The plaintiff shall be entitled to visit the minor children of the parties on the second and fourth Sunday of each month...the visitations shall take place at the home of the husband's sister Mrs. Paul Carter and either Mr. or Mrs. Paul Carter shall be present on the premises at all times..." He can also *"pick the children up at their residence and return them there. [Phil should] transport [the] children by the shortest route and without stop to the Paul Carter residence and return them likewise...to the defendant's residence."*

As I finish reading, I recall that Bonnie Carter was Phil's sister and Paul his brother-in-law. They were in Florida for a time before moving back to Ohio. Grandma had a good relationship with them as well as Don and Gerri, Phil's younger brother and sister-in-law. Don and Gerri continued to maintain a good relationship and visit with Grandma and Grandpa Boreman throughout the years.

In between the legalese of the court documents, I think about my six-year-old dad. Around that time, he had missed weeks of first grade due to stomach ulcers—which, as an adult, he has attributed to his home life during that tumultuous time. I think about the unfair burden of childhood trauma that he and his siblings experienced and how they would carry it with them into adulthood. Grandma was starting over in a new marriage—of which I'm sure she was still testing the waters from having just traded a sober abuser for an alcoholic one.

I pause my ponderings and check my Ancestry inbox. I squeal. It's from Robin Lawrentz! I hope he'll agree to a test. It has only been a week since I asked for his status regarding the DNA test.

"Hello, Allison! I *have* taken the AncestryDNA test. Your dad is not a match with me."

My stomach drops.

Read it again, you're reading it wrong.

I read it again and bite at the hangnail on the edge of my thumb.

Indignant and horrified, I shoot daggers at my screen and try to decide how to respond. There's really nothing else to do besides reach out to Ancestry about the obvious mess up. He and Dad are supposed to be third cousins. He should share *some* DNA with my dad.

A notification for a new Facebook message interrupts my sour fixation with Robin's test. It's from Jen.

"Not sure where to begin, but had lunch with family today... my Aunt Linda clearly remembers your grandparents and your Aunt Linda."

CHAPTER 10

SECRET SISTERS
April, 2017

"Linda immediately knew their names...Your grandparents knew my grandparents, visited each other's homes, etc. My aunt played with your aunt. Our grandmas were friendly. She thinks they met through her dad, (my Grandpa Leon) selling them siding."

Welp. There's no going back now.

No one else Jen had spoken to so far recognized our last name, but Linda did. She remembers *our* Linda and played with her.

I read on slowly. "My biggest concern is [hurting your dad or his siblings]. My aunt does recall that there was a romantic relationship...but Leon had more than one known affair. Leon was *a lot* of trouble, so it would have been a very wise decision to keep him away! I don't want to assume I know what happened for sure...This is so tough because none of the key people are here to tell their story and after all these years...I do not want to cause any hurt feelings. I think you can probably guess what my aunt believes happened...this is not what I expected when I took the DNA test. I was just trying to find out the ethnicity stuff for fun!"

I know what she means. Recreational DNA testing. That's why I had been drawn to it, too. Having done Grandpa Scroggs' test, Grandma Scroggs', Jason's, Dad's...it *was* supposed to be interesting and fun. Enlightening. It's all recreation and games until someone finds out their existence was contingent upon a house needing new siding.

Something in me settles deep and makes itself comfortable. And I'm anything *but* comfortable. How could Grandma keep something like this from us? Is it just my own emotions I'm feeling? Or did I just inherit what emotions may have been some of Grandma's—and what will soon be Dad's?

Is it shame? Betrayal? Foolishness?

No, fear and anger. Maybe not anger. Confusion.

Scratch that—how about all the above. All I know is that things have never seemed so complicated.

Yet, I surrender to the idea that this scenario is the one that makes the most sense. It adds up. And now, I can't unknow it. The lifespan of this secret has come to an end, and I had stopped its sneaky, silently beating heart.

Dad isn't Phil's son, he is Leon's.

How many times did I hear from Dad and his siblings: "Our mom was a saint"? Will she still be a saint in their eyes? How do I even tell my dad? Will he believe me? I didn't mean to find this out. Was it really the ongoing romantic affair as Linda Eckstrom remembered? A one-time mistake? Was it consensual? If Linda recalls that time, who else still living might know something about Grandma's relationship with Leon? So many questions my head hurts.

I consider keeping all of this to myself forever. I could carry on the tradition of secret keeping.

Nope. I'd be awful at it.

Think. Someone living that might know...

Wait. *Mae*!

I write to Jen: "My grandma's best friend is alive and living in Ashland..." What if she remembers the Eckstrom name? And if not, maybe she can recall *something* that could give us a clue.

Easter dinner is here, and I decide to go radio silent when it comes to sharing anything family tree related. I need more time. I was quick to accept Linda's testimony, but will they? Will they say they can't believe someone I only know through the internet? Will they refute the DNA and say it's flat out wrong? No matter how much I try to plan for their questions and anticipate their protests, I resign myself to the fact that revealing this long-buried secret will come with consequences. Whenever it comes to light, there will be consequences. The reality is it is currently my problem to decide if or when and how.

Choosing to keep quiet or tell what I know is surprisingly an easy choice today. It is neither the time nor the place.

I will not be responsible for ruining a perfectly nice Easter. And processing out loud to my dad and our other close family members prematurely could mean being a tour-guide to a full-blown, four-alarm family identity crisis I'm woefully unprepared to take on at the moment.

I make small talk with the relatives starting to gather in my parent's living room and we make our way to the kitchen and dining room. They all seem so happy and content. Just going about their business: it's another season, another family holiday, everything is the same. They all know the same stories, understand the same lineage and heritage just like I did mere days before. Now they are innocent bystanders to the bloodline grenade I could toss into the family tree. I could just chuck it in there and run for cover.

Maybe there is some Family-Secret Burden transfer of power or something I didn't know existed which takes place when another family member (Enter: me) unwittingly unlocks a life-altering secret the original person (Grandma Boreman) was carrying. A magical portal to unleash all the burden of secret-keeping on the unfortunate opener, too curious for their own good.

Just act normal, I remind myself, as I take my seat around the dinner table. My dad says a prayer to bless the meal, and we start buttering rolls and passing the dish of candied carrots and the serving platter of pineapple crowned ham slices. We all dig in and try not to eat too much for the meal; there are plenty of desserts to enjoy later. I grab a couple of colorful hard-boiled eggs from a white bowl in the middle of the table, their swirling bright blues and greens dyed by my children with my mom a few days before. I give them a good crack and focus on peeling them to avoid a mess of teeny eggshell pieces and chunks of perfectly good egg that could join them if I'm not careful.

Jason knows. At some point I will have to bring it up to the people it will directly affect. I expected Jason to plant my feet firmly on the ground and tell me I was overreacting when I explained this new revelation, but even he was convinced. Couldn't my husband have the decency to argue with me and tell me I was completely wrong the one time I needed him to?

My egg-peeling concentration is interrupted by my little sister (yet tallest) sitting across from me. "Hey Ali, have you found out anything else about that girl Sylvia you found a picture of? She looks so much like dad..." she asks, offhandedly taking a swig of her ice water and waiting for my answer.

Panicking, I give an emphatic "Nope!", smother the egg with salt, and shove half of it in my mouth. *No one will suspect a thing.* "Stull lukin' into eht." I say, my cheeks full of iodized-sprinkled, chalky egg as I grab my sweet tea to wash it down.

I glance at my two sisters at the table. I'm the oldest and a redhead. Samantha is the middle—a brunette—while the youngest, Elizabeth is a blonde. I recall a story my mom told us about how a stranger at the grocery store asked her if we all had the same father. Even with our hair color differences, we *never* gave a second thought to the idea of not being fully related to one another.

While we have obvious differences beyond the natural hair color, there is more than just DNA to prove we are full siblings. Our humor, mannerisms, the sound of our voices, how we fight: we're sisters.

But say my daughter came to me when I was pushing 58 and told me she was sure the two sisters I had were actually my half-sisters, and oh, by the way, you have an additional seven—SEVEN—more sisters because your dad really isn't your dad...well, I don't even know how I'd respond.

I imagine I'd have a lot of questions.

CHAPTER 11

MAE DAY
April, 2017

 I knock on the door of the wheat-colored apartment, and a woman I don't recognize is standing in front of me. With both of us confused, I start to explain. "Hi, I'm looking for Mae..."

"Oh!" she says, her puzzled expression quickly turns into a friendly smile. "She's right next door." As I thank her and turn down the short sidewalk, the door of the apartment duplex I failed to choose opens and an elderly lady in a button-down striped shirt and brown slacks greets me.

"I'm over here!" She laughs. "Hi, Ali! Come on in!" The late spring sun is warm and comforting but I'm on a mission that can only happen inside this home. The extra Vitamin D will have to wait.

"It's great to see you, Mae! It's been a long time!" Her apartment is small, but it's all she needs. "How are you doing?"

"Oh, I'm managing! I'm so glad you came over!" She motions for me to sit at her dine-in kitchen table. "How's your mom and dad doin'?"

I sit like I'm told to and place the white bakery box of our local grocery store's donuts on the table as a treat for us both. If anyone can help me put the pieces together, it will be Mae.

At eighty-nine, she is still getting around alright and has a sharp memory. I think the last time I saw her was at Grandma's funeral and then prior to that, at my wedding in 2006. Jason and I had gone pew by pew in the sanctuary to greet our guests and dismiss them to the reception.

When I got to Grandma and her "plus one," I hugged them both. Our photographer captured the moment—just the wrong half of the moment. The photograph shows Jason and I post-hug and smiling with Mae while Grandma, wearing her Pepto-Bismol pink top and matching skirt is slightly hidden. Her small frame peeking out from behind us, politely waiting for her friend to join her and drive her home.

The week before our visit, I called Mae hoping she'd remember me and was happy to find she did. I explained I wanted to visit with her, bring a few pictures, and ask her some questions about Grandma I thought she might be able to help me with. We set a date and time to visit. She was as gracious and kind as I had remembered her being.

Our initial chit-chatting winds down and the conversation naturally turns to Grandma.

"I was the only one she told about the abuse—back then you just didn't say anything about it. There wasn't much you could do."

Fast forward a couple of years to when Grandma and Grandpa Boreman were first married, and he was still drinking heavily. Because of Pete's possessiveness over her, Evelyn wasn't allowed to be in contact with Mae. Family lore has it Grandma whacked him over the head with a frying pan and gave him an ultimatum, along with a goose egg.

"Whadja do that for!?" He cried.

"It's the bottle or us!" She declared.

Apparently, it had done the trick and knocked the desire for alcohol right out of him. The curse of inebriation had been broken with Teflon and some Evelyn moxie. I was told Grandpa started going to church with them and cleaned up his act.

It wasn't long before Grandma and Mae reconnected and picked up their friendship where they left off.

Mae shares memories and stories and reminds me of their visiting/shopping day they aptly named "Mae Day." I'm thankful Grandma had such an amazing lifelong friend. Like the rest of our family, she noticed Grandma's depression worsening toward the end.

Mae sighs. "Some days she was really down; she didn't feel like doing anything or going anywhere."

Of course, what I am really hoping for is for Mae to confirm the Leon/Evelyn relationship. Because she is recalling memories from the late 1940's and early 1950's in such detail, I feel confident something will trigger a recollection. I begin delicately, but to the point.

"Mae, recently I had Dad take one of those DNA tests...you know, where you have to spit into a tube...and I was curious...well, there's a name I never heard of before that popped up as a match for him, and I thought maybe you'd be able to shed some light on it." Watching her body language, she doesn't seem avoidant; in fact, she seems intrigued. I continue.

"So, the last name of the family I'm wondering about is Eckstrom...first names are Leon and Wilma. Do you happen to remember them being around Grandma and Phil, or even your own family?" She looks in the direction of the past to think and scrunches her eyebrows together. I keep my breathing short and as silent as I can; I dare not say a word to disrupt her concentration. It seems like minutes, but only a couple of seconds have passed.

"Hmmm, can't say that rings a bell...but I don't have many bells left to ring!" She laughs and I force a smile but am disappointed. She may be my only living connection to Grandma and that time period as an adult, and she doesn't know the secret either. Without much of a break in conversation, she continues.

"You know, your grandma's family was from Georgia..."

How do I get back on topic now without being too pushy? I am half-listening while I think. She didn't just pull a fast one on me, did she? Sweet Mae? No. She'd tell me if she knew. But I don't push the subject. She either doesn't know or is not going to let on she does.

Say Mae does know. She knew Grandma longer than anyone else and she is being a dear, loyal friend by keeping her late friend's secret for her. I can respect that. But there's got to be a way to wear an 89-year-old lady down without putting her at a desk and shining bright lights in her eyes.

The tea she made us is still hot. I take a bigger swig than normal so I don't accidentally blurt out anything I shouldn't. Given the recent findings, however, it could jog her memory or encourage her admit to what she knows. But the timing doesn't feel right.

I get back to asking her safer questions about Grandma and those early years. We look at a few pictures together and she shares a few stories of her own life experiences. She's not my Grandma, but she's the closest thing I've got to her now. Even though she's a lot like her, Mae is her own person. Independent and ambitious, funny and kind; Mae has a beautiful story of courage and resilience all her own. Her life is woven into a part of my family's story just as Evelyn's life was woven into hers.

Later that day, I process the time I spent with Mae and second guess the questions I asked her. My mind wanders back to the old Lawrentz cabin we visited in West Virginia ten years earlier. That old home, covered by aluminum siding for the last few decades, was being taken apart right in front of our eyes when we got there. A skeleton structure. The old logs exposed, light hitting their knots and grains once again. Even in that exposure, and thinking I understood what it revealed to us about our family—about who we were—there was *still* a truth hidden from us.

Before something new can be built, the old must be torn down. The family tree I had carefully built out name by name, date by date with Lawrentz ancestors, was being dismantled along with the log cabin. Someone will take its remains and move it to a new location and rebuild it there. But it doesn't belong to us anymore. It never had.

The idea that reality had been staring back at us long before we laid eyes on the West Virginia cabin haunts me. Ghosts watching us, their very presence whispering the truth while we live our lives unknown to our very selves. It peers at us in mirrors, pumps through our veins, and lies locked inside our DNA.

But the truth is also tucked into boxes in my basement, the contents of which I thought I knew, and now they seem like they belong in *The Tell-Tale Heart.* Unlike Poe's story, I had *unknowingly* placed it underneath my house.

Secrets are the things we can't face in the moment and want to get rid of—so we bury them alive. We think we are destroying the knowledge somehow, or it will quiet down on its own and be forgotten. We hope maybe they'll be lost after our own deaths.

Even if someone finds the secrets that remain, we hope they won't understand the significance. Eventually someone will hear a faint pulse and the stirring—the cry—of the tell-tale *secret.* After hibernating for some time, secrets wait for the right season to emerge through the dark earth reaching for the light. To be seen.

Did more truth still wait in my basement bins and boxes? Or in the crowded storage units left untouched for years?

How can something this foundational to our existence be hiding from us for 58 years? Was it waiting for the right moment to be revealed? It feels like she is leading me to the truth. Or God is. They both are. Maybe Evelyn and Wilma and God were all leading Jen and I to discover the truth.

I know deep down I'm called to be a finder and connector of lost things. And a truth teller. But there is a strange temptation to obey the deceiving yet enchanting life of the cycle of secrets—a siren song to protect the story at all costs. It invites me to seal the box up tight and shovel another pile of glistening dirt right on top.

AncestryDNA tests are finally on sale, so I place my order for the kits. One for Uncle Jim and one for Uncle Frank. My teeth clench at the thought of everything that has come to light in such a short time since asking them to test. But there's no looking back. We need the results now more than ever. I let my uncles know the order was made, and I wait.

The tests will take a week or two to be delivered. I try to forget about it, but it's nearly impossible. A week crawls by. I do my daily check of the mail and finally: a tower of white and green plastic-wrapped boxes is stacked underneath the mailbox on our porch. No long suffering in the wait, but it means it's now my turn to deliver, and this time to the test takers. There may still be suffering yet. I try to keep calm.

The kids will be out of school in a couple hours. Without much more thought (and before I chicken out), I jump in my mini-van and head to Hawkins Bakery. Apparently buttering people up by bestowing them with gifts of fried dough is a new technique of mine. If they behave themselves, I muse, I will hand over the apple fritters and bear claws.

After success at the bakery counter, I head out to the office. I pull into the parking lot, eyes half-closed, praying for a smooth saliva-to-tube transfer. I grab the test kits, my purse, and any courage I have and head through the front entrance. Around the hallway to the right of the front doors I poke my head into my mom's office.

"Hi! I have some presents for Uncle Jim and Uncle Frank."

She smiles. "The donuts or the boxes?" We chat for a minute, and it gives me a chance to calm my nerves. Mom and Dad both knew I had been looking more closely into the Lawrentz side lately and had wanted to compare everyone I could using DNA, so while *my* nerves were fraying, they had no cause for alarm. I head toward the opposite end of the hallway to say a quick hello to my dad.

"Hi, Sweetie!" he says, seeing me walk in. If not my name, it was usually "Sweetie," "Kiddo," or "Red." The nicknames of my childhood aren't used anymore, like "Gumba" and "Alibaba." He stands to give me a hug and a peck on the cheek.

I can smell the leather-bound planner and his briefcase that would make a sharp clink when he opened it. The abrupt snap of the shiny metal latch would always surprise me and make me wince a little—I have always kept my fingers away from it at all costs. As a kid, I'd see my dad with his Franklin Planner and the briefcase full of faxes, letterhead, presentation folders, sell sheets, and dot matrix printer paper, and I knew he had to be someone very important. Always the driven person, my dad has an unwavering work ethic and an immovable sense of duty, integrity, and dedication—sometimes to a fault.

A small collection of pens sits on the desk. A couple of them are those really fancy kinds that professional businessmen have for signing official documents. There are houseplants, books, trinkets from Father's Days past, framed photos of all of us including the grandkids at various ages lining the office bookshelves and his desk. A couple of mounted Walleye hang on the wall, with the weight and length of the fish as well as his name and date of the Lake Erie catches engraved on the brass "Fish Ohio" plaques positioned directly under each one.

The TV mounted in the corner adjacent to the fish is on like usual, with a news show debating the hot political topics of the day. He invites me to set my things down at the small oak table just under the TV, and I offer him a donut before I set out on my mission.

Armed with the two tests and box of donuts, I head into Uncle Jim's office first, then Uncle Frank's, both right across the hall. I affirm my decision to not only drop off the kits but hang around until they finish them so I can immediately make a beeline to the post office.

I put on my "mom" face, instructing each of them how to go about it and double checking they hadn't eaten or drank anything within the last half hour.

"When you're done, I will give you your donut as your reward," I joke.

Uncle Jim opens the kit and I head out the door to let him spit in peace. Next to Uncle Frank's office to start the process once more. In both offices the jokes are flying.

"This will prove I'm adopted!" and "So this isn't a urine sample, right?"

They each write me a reimbursement check, even though I told them it's on me. I had offered to cover the cost because they were helping me out. They insist and I accept it anyway; 'cause I'm no dummy. Their ethnicity results will just be a fun bonus they get to share with family. I still hang onto a tiny sliver of hope it will clear everything up, and maybe there is a perfectly reasonable explanation to all the recent weirdness I haven't considered yet.

I glance at the check that a chuckling Uncle Frank had given me and am brought back to reality. I want to laugh, but it hits too close to home.

In the memo line he had written *Paternity Test.*

With vials of spit sealed tightly in envelopes, Operation Donut-Drop & Spit-Retrieval is complete. Time to get out of here before I lose whatever cool I have. The sinking feeling of getting away with something once again comes over me.

Why do I feel guilty? Some unseen force wants this shut down. Forget what I saw, what I heard, what I know. *She knows too much; who does she think she is?* I hear it whisper, around hidden corners, behind darkened windows, within the chemicals of developed photos, and within the memory of my own DNA.

Shutting off my autopilot brain, I remember to not head home. I go straight to the post office, drive through drop off, and place the kits carefully in the slot—listening to them both as they slide down the chute and make a thud on top of other people's envelopes and packages in that blue metal box.

Now I wait.

⁂

All three brothers worked together before. They worked for a good man named Bruce in a brick office building and warehouse in Mansfield. Bruce was the second-generation owner of a company and a great mentor to Dad, not to mention a grandfather-like figure to us three girls. I think he loved us like granddaughters. All these years later a canvas print he gave me of Monet's *Resting Under the Lilacs* hangs in my house, and a copy of *Madeline* by Ludwig Bemelmans still sits on my bookshelf. He passed away not too long ago.

For as many poor male role models as my dad had in his life, there were a handful of ones who were forces of positivity and encouragement. His grandfather Frank Bowers being at the top of his list. One from his childhood was Joe Wilson, one of Grandma's attorneys. Then in his late 20's and all of his 30's was Bruce. Dad knew he wanted to do something that took brains, and these men were not only good men, but smart, hardworking men. He could imagine himself in their shoes. These men earned his trust and respect, while others had not.

Dad worked his way up to General Manager. He had the intelligence and motivation to help the company succeed. He traveled the world—Britain, Italy, Turkey, South Korea, Thailand—and continued to learn and grow not only as a salesman and business manager within the industry, but about world trade and developing meaningful customer relationships. Many of those customers have turned into lifelong friendships. He worked so hard and was respected by other employees because of his integrity, business skills, and innovation. His standard of excellence and his bar of expectation were set high.

In my search for records about Leon Eckstrom, I had been glancing at the photos and names of those students in his class from the 1940 Mansfield Senior High yearbook. The name of someone I knew jumped out at me. I gasped. It was my dad's former boss and mentor, Bruce. He had been in the very same graduating class as Leon.

It felt like a fated connection; Dad having him as a close mentor, unaware that Bruce, at the very least, knew of the father Dad never realized he had.

Did Bruce ever say in passing to his young protégé, *"You remind me of this fellow I went to high school with... he was a redhead and a salesman, too..."*?

Dad would have shrugged at the name Leon Eckstrom.

It wouldn't have rung any bells.

CHAPTER 12

LET'S GET TOGETHER

April, 2017

"For everything hidden is meant to be revealed,
and everything concealed is meant to be brought to light."
MARK 4:22

The 1961 movie *The Parent Trap* starred Hayley Mills, Maureen O'Hara, Brian Keith—and Hayley Mills. This Disney live action film was based on a 1940's German book proposed under the name *The Great Secret,* and then called *Lottie & Lisa* by Erich Kästner.

My Grandpa Boreman introduced my sisters and I to it when we were little, and I adored it. They had recorded it to a VHS tape from a TV special for us which was then played dozens of times; I was enamored with Sharon and even practiced talking like her. I loved how brave and rough and tumble Susan was and how she lived in California and rode horses. I memorized the feature song "Let's Get Together" and tried to play it on the piano, since I had been taking lessons from a retired lady in my neighborhood. Each Tuesday after school, I'd ride my pink and purple Huffy from the north side of our street to the south side where she lived.

What intrigued me most about *The Parent Trap* was how these two girls, separated at birth, met on a whim at summer camp. Being drawn to each other by some force—even fighting like siblings—and then putting two and two together: they belonged to each other.

"Don't you feel it? Don't you know what's happening? Don't you find it peculiar that we're so alike and have the same birthday?"

"It's just one of those things…isn't it?"

Coincidence or maybe serendipity?

"Mother says I'm psychic. That I can sense when something odd is going to happen. I always get goosebumps. Look." Sharon continued, *"I believe fate brought us together."*

Sounds Sharondipitous to me.

I'll be here all night, folks.

The two sisters went to work planning how they would trick their divorced parents into getting back together. The divorcees had each taken one baby girl to live with them, splitting them up and never telling them about the existence of the other twin. I guess it makes for an entertaining movie, but seems like an ill-conceived parenting choice for real-life.

But Maureen O'Hara and Brian Keith aside from their questionable parenting? Dreamy.

Susan learned how to be a bit more proper so she could return to Boston and meet their mother while Sharon chopped off her hair and learned how to be a bit sassier so she could go back to California and meet their father.

While at the family's California ranch, Sharon meets Verbena, the housekeeper who incessantly mumbles, *"None of my never mind…I'm not saying a word. Not one single word."* A few people learn about the twins meeting at camp and now try to keep this revelation of uncovering the secret—well, secret. Ultimately, no matter how many secrets develop from that initial decision to make an event secret, the truth reveals itself.

🐝

The next step in my search should be to raid my basement and dig through the large plastic bins full of photo albums and scrapbooks. So downstairs I go to find any physical proof that corroborates Linda

Eckstrom's memory with the DNA connecting my dad, Jen, Susie, and Josh.

I pull up a couple of bins at a time into the living room as a start. If I can systematically pour through everything I have of hers, I may come across a few needles of proof in the haystacks of items she kept.

It's the perfect day to sit out on my porch, so I pull one scrapbook, one album, a box of postcards, and head out the front door—kids following me like ducklings. School is out for the day.

"Hey, what's all that?" My long-time neighbor and friend Heather is on her porch, book in hand. I smile.

"I just brought up some old stuff to look at!"

"Ooh!" she calls out. "Want some help?"

"Sure!" I shout back, welcoming the help and her company.

She puts down the book she's reading and makes her way to the sidewalk and up the front steps to my porch, her little duckling following her. Heather already knows what "old stuff" I'm referring to. A few days before, I couldn't help but fill her in on a little bit of the developing story.

"Here's a box of postcards if you want to just look for any names with 'Leon' or 'Wilma' on them—the last name is Eckstrom...And while you're flipping through those, I'll go through this scrapbook."

We cringe at some of the postcards in the collection for their sexist or racist tones and laugh at others for their ridiculous jokes. Some have wonderful mid-century typefaces and graphics, and some are just photographs of places all over the world. Quite the collection.

"Is this something? A person named Hal—"

I interrupt her, "Oh, no, I'm sure that's just my Great Uncle Harold, we call him Buzz, I guess sometimes he would go by Hal as a young man..." We continue flipping through our assigned items, sharing interesting bits of writing or images and looking up every so often to see what our ornery kids are up to. Even with being in school all day, to our amazement they stay fully energized. Up on the porch with us, then in the yard, sidewalk, garage, then back up and back down again.

After setting the kids up with some Goldfish crackers, Heather and I replant ourselves on my Amish-made solid-wood porch swing and sit side by side. Captivated by the variety of things Grandma pasted inside the scrapbooks, not even the mildew odor and brittle paper phases me. But I don't have time to lollygag. I refocus and try to look for anything which would point to Grandma knowing this family—a family of strangers to me these decades later. Most likely she'd have gotten rid of any evidence I will find helpful. Intentionally or unintentionally.

Heather brings the porch swing to an abrupt halt and the chains give a sharp clunk and clang together in response.

"Eck...Eck-strum...Eckstrom? Is that it? Is that the name we're looking for?" She victoriously holds up a postcard with a 1960 postmark addressed to "Mr. & Mrs. L.G. Eckstrom".

CHAPTER 13

CAUGHT RED-HEADED

April, 2017

Heather quickly hands me the postcard. There it is. *Eckstrom.* Almost breathless, I carefully inspect the 57-year-old piece of mail. I note the address, the date it was postmarked, and record it in my notebook. The written greeting is from their daughter, Carol (the oldest of the seven girls), while on her honeymoon with her new husband.

"Why would your grandma have this when it's not even to or from her?" Heather asks. I explain that it would be reasonable to assume that Wilma gave my grandma the postcard because of her collection hobby. She not only had a postcard collection but saved stamps and postmarks as well.

A whole section of a scrapbook I have is filled with cut out postmarks, organized by state. It's not at all strange to me that she had a piece of mail addressed to someone else; but to find the name Eckstrom on something the first day I decide to start digging? I'm floored.

I now have:

a.) scientific proof (DNA)

b.) eyewitness proof (Linda's story)

c.) physical proof (postcard)

I pull out my phone and take a picture of the front and back as an additional safeguard, still on a high from such an incredible find.

The postcard is in good condition with a stamp that has a postmark of June 7, 1960, from Mount Morris, Michigan. The front of the card shows a photograph from Saginaw, Michigan. On the back Carol writes about their trip and how she would see her parents Leon and Wilma that coming weekend.

Mr. & Mrs. L.G. Eckstrom
166 Ridge Road
Mansfield, Ohio

All the what-ifs flood my mind.

Had I not known to look for that name, the postcard would be just another card in her collection. Maybe we would sort through them one day and throw away all the ones that weren't from family or weren't deemed important. What if sorting never happened at all? The whole box could have been trashed in any one of the many moves the family had in the last six decades.

But it made it to *my* basement. A single 3.5" x 5" piece of cardstock. Out of all the other adult children and cousins' homes or storage units it could have been kept in.

My runaway thoughts are interrupted by Heather, who had obviously been motivated to continue the search while I remained entranced by the unexpected gift of the postcard.

"Look, another Eckstrom card!"

She passes me a second postcard: again, from Carol to her parents during her honeymoon trip. Jen is going to flip. Postcards that my grandma had in her collection from Jen's Aunt Carol—*our* Aunt Carol.

This one is postmarked in Canada. Carol's scrawled note in cursive starts off: *"Gee, but this is a marvelous place."*

Before I can read any further, Heather struck gold again. A *third* postcard. They must have been grouped together when Grandma initially collected them for us to find one after the other. How thoughtful of her.

"Ali, look at this...This one is also addressed to the Eckstroms, but the message is all scribbled out..." She hands me the vintage postcard that features Los Angeles, its concrete jungle of roads and exit ramps intertwining and looping every which way. I'm sure the photo was supposed to tout an impressive infrastructure feat of mid-century America. But postcards should make you want to travel to the place shown on the front. This M.C. Escher-esq paved-paradise of a highway wasn't doing it for me.

I flip to the back. It doesn't match Carol's handwriting. *Maybe Grandma's?* I notice this card has no stamp, no residual glue, no postmark—it was never sent. Same address as the other postcards: the Eckstrom residence on Ridge Road in Mansfield.

Is Los Angeles significant? Who scribbled out the message? The same person who wrote it? And why scribble it out in the first place, but keep the postcard? I am determined to read it anyway. I strain my eyes, squinting and blinking to focus but I can only make out the first word: "Howdy".

My grandma always said "Howdy" when we came over. Did she go to L.A.? I never heard her mention ever going to California. She never really traveled at all, at least not that I know of. She didn't drive, and the only "traveling" I can think she may have done back in those days would have been family road trips south to see Georgia family. And I *never* remembered hearing about her flying on a plane anywhere.

Phil had been to more places. He was in the Air National Guard, I remind myself, so he could have gotten the postcard from Mansfield Lahm Airport...or from a buddy, and Grandma just used it to send a note on.

Wait.

Phil and Grandma's marriage record. I found it a long time ago in an online search. It has both of their signatures on it; I could compare those with this postcard's writing and maybe I can tell if it's either of theirs.

Heather and I cut the investigation short to start getting ready for dinner. I thank her and we say goodbye to each other as I start inside, bringing with me the three smoking guns. But the magnetic pull of discovery is strong. Food can be prepped after I consult a vital record first. Just one.

At my home office desk (AKA the former dining room) I pull up the digitized version of their marriage record on my laptop, and with the mystery postcard in hand, a quick glance at how the capital "L" and the capital "R" are formed instantly gives me my answer.

I bounce out of my office chair, walk the five steps from the kitchen and flip on our bright ceiling fan light. Hovering over our small Formica mid-century table with chrome legs, I hold the postcard up to the light, straining my eyes once again to see. This time, in the light, I can read the words fully. I pause on each word, holding my breath like I might blow the words away and never get them back.

The handwriting belongs to *Phil*.

He wrote the following brief and unfinished message:

"Howdy—1st, thanks Leon for taking Evie to Airport"

I sigh out all my air. Now I am deeper down the rabbit hole. Grandma hadn't thrown it out, but she—or someone—had scribbled out the message and left who it was addressed to.

Was Phil already in L.A. so Leon took her to the airport to catch a plane and fly out there? Whose idea was it? Surely one of her parents or brothers or Mae could have taken her. Was my dad born yet? There is no date on the card of any kind. It looks like an early 1960's style, but I want to know for sure. The only clue I have is the Eckstrom's Ridge Road address. I don't think they lived very long at this particular place. From Jen's comments and city directories I leafed through, they may have only been there from 1960 to 1961 before they moved south to Columbus.

If that is when Phil wrote it, then my dad would have been less than a year old. The families were still connecting with each other even after my dad's birth. In my mind, once Grandma realized she was pregnant, she would have avoided the Eckstrom's like the plague for fear of anyone suspecting her baby wasn't Phil's. Maybe she figured doing that would have added more suspicion than to continue seeing them? Or could Linda Eckstrom be right? Had there been a continued romantic affair going on?

If Dad *was* born before this ride to the airport, would he have gone with her? Stayed behind with my great-grandparents? Did Leon know this little red-headed boy was his? Did Wilma know? Did Grandma? She had to have known, right? She at least had to consider the possibility. *I'll just name the baby Phillip,* maybe she thought. *Phillip Michael Lawrentz. Just to remove any doubt.*

Oh, Grandma. You knew I loved family history and your pictures and scrapbooks. You and others gave me boxes full of those things, knowing I would take care of them, scan them, and share them. Did you ever think I would find clues to your secrets? Did you secretly hope I would?

Forcing myself to take a break after the exhausting barrage of thoughts, I wonder about the Evelyn I obviously don't know at all. That no one in my family knows. I stick the three postcards in a safe place and try to focus on making dinner.

CHAPTER 14

SOUVENIRS

May, 2017

The morning light hits the pothos hanging in my kitchen window seat. How does it get layered with dust so fast? I know I should get a damp cloth and shine up the leaves, but I gently run each one through three fingers and a thumb, sending the dust onto the throw pillow and the floor. I'll ignore it for now.

The scent of soil plus any green growing thing makes me excited for each spring and summer's gardening season. Hands in dirt, placing new plants in, and being surprised at the forgotten perennials planted in seasons past. Remembering who gave me each start and what joy every plant brings during the summer. It's a similar feeling to pulling out Christmas ornaments from boxes each year.

I shouldn't even look over at the jade plant sitting on the bay window above the sink. I look anyway. Dusty. Jade leaves are trickier. So fragile and so many. I do the same lazy technique I do to the pothos, but just a leaf between my pointer finger and thumb. One breaks off and I let it drop to the soil. Maybe it will regenerate, or maybe it will rot.

Plant polishing is not in my usual morning routine. I grab day-old coffee from the fridge and place it in the microwave. I only have a couple more hours until I need to pick up Clementine from preschool. I fix myself a bowl of Special K Vanilla Almond cereal and set out some new items to study. Coffee is ready. I settle into my kitchen chair and look at two postcards I previously set aside. They stood out because of their 1959 date.

I start to realize that each time I understand a new piece of the puzzle, I have to go back through things I've seen before. Boxes I've already pored over before, pictures already studied—because with that new bit of information, it's now a new lens through which to see everything.

This is going to take a while.

The two postcards I'm now studying seem to go together, like they are from the same trip. Grandma wrote both. The Ponticana Cafe in Tifton, Georgia, card seems to be first in the timeline. "Home of good coffee and famous for its Western Steaks and Chops" is printed on the back top left corner. It's written to a nine-year-old Linda Lawrentz.

> *"Hi Linny, this is where we ate breakfast Sunday a.m. I got your letter today (Monday) glad to hear from you. I got one arm sunburned hanging it out the window. It finally quit raining. It's hot and sticky. I sort of miss our cold weather. Leon isn't down yet he just called from Atlanta where he's waiting for a plane to come on down. Wesley is taller than I am now! Charlene has grown, too. Will stop and write Jimbo now.*
> *Love, Mom"*

In a method I'm sure is not a scientific or journalistic one, I examine the card and run down through things I understand and things I don't.

1. Jimbo: Uncle Jim
2. Charlene and Wesley: Phil's sister Bonnie and her husband Paul's two kids; they lived in Lakeland, Florida. She must have written it in Florida at Bonnie's house then if she's talking about her kids.
3. Leon isn't down yet he just called from Atlanta where he's waiting for a plane to come on down: *Leon?*

But which one?

Oddly enough I now know of *two* Leons in this mess. I mustn't forget that Grandma had an Uncle Leon who was married to her mother's sister. They lived in Georgia. Is she referring to him? Maybe. But why would he *fly* down to mid Florida to see them while they are visiting with Phil's family? If he was supposed to meet them for some reason, wouldn't he just drive the few hours south? They would have easily gone right past the Bowers/England residences to see them before they got to Florida—they could have even picked her uncle up on the way. Plus, Grandma was writing to her daughter, not another adult, and Linda was only nine years old at the time. Wouldn't she have referred to him as *Uncle* Leon if it was their family member? Was visiting Phil's sister and family really the purpose of being in Florida?

I know things have probably changed: roads, cars, and speed limits. But maybe Google Maps can give me an idea on distance and time to answer part of the question? I plug in all the places.

Ashland, Ohio, all the way to Lakeland, Florida, is 1,112 miles one way. Around 17 hours of driving. What would keep Phil and Evelyn from taking a plane like they would in 1960? Then there's Rossville, Georgia, near the Tennessee state line where her relatives are from, including Uncle Leon and Aunt Lucille (England) Cain. On trips throughout the years to visit the Georgia relatives, they would drive the short distance to Lookout Mountain, see the Tennessee River and other beautiful sites around the area. But I-40 South turns into I-75 and takes them right through Rossville, through Atlanta and all the way down to Tifton before crossing into Florida. Rossville to Tifton was about four hours. Then 75 takes them all the way to Lakeland. An additional four hours. *And how much did it cost to fly back then? These families didn't have money growing on trees. And why didn't they just bring Uncle Leon with them if he was planning to come to Florida as well?* I suppose he could have flown, given Rossville to Lakeland was an eight-hour drive. But the question remains, why? Did that make sense for Uncle Leon to be the Leon referenced in the postcard? Or was it more likely Leon Eckstrom was taking a flight from Ohio to Florida with a connecting flight in Atlanta to meet his new friends for some reason? Maybe he had some business first in The Big Peach.

The next postcard *did* have a date. This time Grandma writes to Don and Gerri Lawrentz, Phil's brother and sister-in-law, with the postmark of early March 1959. She waited to get back to Ashland to send it. She writes:

> *"Tuesday 11 a.m. We left Florida about 9:30 last night and are in Atlanta now. Phil and Leon are looking at "a job" and I'm sitting in the car. I've been awake since Monday 7 a.m. so will make this short.*
> *Love, Eve & Phil"*

"A job"? Why was "a job" in quotes? Maybe I'm reading too much into it. She could be subtly sarcastic at times—maybe she had little hope for it to pan out. Was Phil looking for employment halfway between his sister and Evelyn's extended family? Did they have plans to move the whole family down to Georgia or Florida? Why was Leon (either one) involved?

One more clue. A *third* postcard.

This was also for Don and Gerri; only it was from Bonnie, Phil and Don's sister. Another perspective from Grandma and Phil's visit while they were still in Florida. She dates it 2/17 and it has a postmark of February 18, 1959.

> *"Hi, you all. I'm keeping Evie busy. Paul and Phil went fishing today. The kids are fine. Phil sure looks heavier, Evie stays about the same. We are going golfing tonite. Paul is taking us to Miami Fri. Hope everyone is ok. Looking forward to coming home in June.*
> *Love Paul, Bonnie & Kiddies"*

No mention of a Leon.

I locate the photos easily.

A couple of prints of Grandma and Phil at different distances from the camera, and a few duplicates where someone had cut Phil out of the photos. The wide shot shows the two of them standing under an overhang with the words *"SOUVENIRS • INDIAN CRAFTS"* at an outdoor tourist market. Large, ornate handmade rugs and dresses, some with

February 14-26 1959

Saturday, February 14, 1959
Evelyn & Phil leave Ohio for Florida.

Sunday, February 15, 1959
Breakfast at the Ponciana Cafe in Tifton, Georgia.

Monday, February 16, 1959
Evelyn writes postcard to Linda. Made it to Lakeland, FL, "Leon" just called from Atlanta waiting on a plane to "come on down".

Tuesday, February 17, 1959
Paul takes Phil fishing, then Paul, Bonnie, Phil, and Evelyn go golfing

Wednesday, February 18, 1959
Bonnie's postcard is postmarked on this date.

Friday, February 20, 1959
Paul and Bonnie Carter planned to take Evie and Phil to Miami.

Monday, February 23, 1959
Evelyn & Phil leave Florida 9:30 PM.

Tuesday, February 24, 1959
Postcard from Evelyn written 11 AM to Don and Gerri Lawrentz from Atlanta. Phil and Leon are looking at "a job" there.

Thursday, February 26, 1959
Possibly arrive back in Ashland, Ohio.

peacocks on them, hang in a row behind them like a backdrop. Printed on the photos: FEB 1959. I imagine it would be a place in the mountain area between Tennessee, Georgia, and North Carolina. *So who took the picture for them? A stranger? One of the Leons?*

Here's what's now playing ad nauseam inside my head: around nine months later, Evelyn would give birth to an 8lb.12oz. red-headed baby boy.

Nine months later.

Howdy, there Mike.

My whole life he's been the dad who has known everything. He could have gone on *Jeopardy* and won. He'd be my pick for a lifeline on *Who Wants to Be a Millionaire.* He's the right person if you had to pair up in teams for Trivial Pursuit. But it's not the first time I told him something he didn't already know.

Four years ago, in 2013, I had followed up on some Lawrentz searching and found a new vital record I hadn't seen before. A Social Security Death Index record for Phil. He had died back in October of 2011.

I was a little conflicted at the time on whether to deliver the information. He had struggled with the memory and complexity of a relationship with this man that abused them, hurt their mom, and forgiveness was complicated. He understood Phil as a biological father who didn't fight to get better and be the dad they needed. Hope of any parental attachment for his real dad had long since passed, maybe never really existed, and he accepted Pete filling that role for he and his siblings. But even in the most estranged parental relationship, you'd want to be told if the person that made up half of you had died, right?

I told my mom what I found. "Should I tell him?" I asked. She seemed to think it would be okay. So one Saturday morning after brunch around their dining room table, I told him Phil had died. I thought it might bring some closure at least. I remember him saying he had wondered if he'd ever be faced with speaking to him again—he wondered what he'd say—and he decided that it just made him very uneasy. "Now," he had said that morning in 2013, "I guess I don't have to worry about that anymore."

This is it.

You are going to tell your Dad tonight, I command myself, *no weaseling out of it.* As the hour gets closer, throwing up seems like a good option. Jason and I decide that when we come back to pick the kids up from my parents' house, he will just take them home with him so I can stay behind. We drive separately. My body continues to remind me how terrible at compartmentalizing I am. If the secret was hoping to stay hidden, it chose the wrong descendant to find a home in.

We let ourselves in as usual and no matter how hard I try to act natural, I'm sure they can see right through me.

I begin to more fully understand why you bury a secret as significant as this one. If you wear it near the surface, always just about to speak it out loud, it will make you so uncomfortable that the alternative is to push it way down deep. You have a default instinct to keep quiet.

You start to believe its whispers that letting it out will just create pain and do more harm to yourself and others. *Act like it never happened,* it says.

Even though I can't unknow it, I have a choice: share a complicated and potentially destructive secret or keep my family in the dark and save them from any pain the knowledge of it could bring. I'd be doing everyone a kindness.

In the living room, we make our typical conversation of how the kids behaved, if they ate all their dinner, what one-liners the sassy little redhead said this time.

"Okay, kids, let's go," says Jason. "Mom's going to hang back with Grandma and Grandpa for a few minutes." I glance toward my parents' confused faces and add, "Yeah, we drove separately. I just want to show you something. It shouldn't take long."

The kids give hugs, and they are out the door. I try to ignore the lump in my throat and the twisting in my stomach.

My mom dives right in, sensing something is weird. "Are you and Jason okay?" I know I have zero poker face, but I don't even have my shoes off yet.

"If by 'okay,' you mean: did I remember to pick up Diet Coke at the store again? Then no!" I laugh and reassure them while I buy time and pick up my tote bag that contains the entirety of my investigation plus a Michelob Ultra I bought for my dad just for the occasion.

"Can we go into the dining room and sit at the table?" They agree and follow me through the kitchen uncharacteristically quiet. Dad takes his seat at the head of the table, and I grab the spot to his left. Instead of sitting, my mom grabs three cups and fills them with ice water, offers me some leftover dessert she served the kids after dinner, and finally sits down.

Things are in motion now; I'm going to spill the beans whether the secret is ready for me to or not. The first thing I grab out of my bag is the bottle of beer and I place it in front of my dad. He bursts into laughter. "It's that bad, is it? Or are we celebrating something?" I feel a little more at ease hearing his laugh, even though my insides are still at Olympic gymnast level, and I have a heart that is pounding in my ear drums. I pull out the white three-ring binder I began only a couple months prior, filled with all the evidence of the search. Each item or paper is tucked inside a plastic sheet and carefully organized.

Deep down I know they won't be angry with me, but I consider new problems. What if they want to keep it between us—and continue the cycle of secret keeping? What if they think I just got it wrong and had some unfounded hunch and forced it into fact? The last thing I wanted in the world was for my dad to think I was completely illogical or for my mom to think I was just being dramatic and making a big deal over nothing.

Snap out of it. Your goal is to just present the facts in a calm, clear manner. I am an adult after all. Not some high-drama, jump-to-conclusions kind of teenage girl. At least, I'm not anymore. Something about being alone with your parents in a location where you spent a lot of time with them as a kid instantly transports you back to being a juvenile. My reputation precedes me, and during those angst-ridden years these two were witness to it all.

Like the moment—only a few feet away from our current spots at the table—when I, a mere thirteen-year-old lass, sat on the kitchen floor in tears and begged them to let me go to the theater to see *Titanic* for a fourth time. "You don't understand!" I wailed.

But that was then. This is now. Now is DNA data, matches and charts, census records, timelines, aluminum siding, and for my final trick, some genealogical pyrotechnics.

I start from the beginning. Not far into my slow-moving presentation my mom interrupts me.

"His dad isn't Phil!" She shouts it like she hit the buzzer and is first to solve a bonus round puzzle on *Wheel of Fortune.* The hum of the fridge is all I hear for what feels like a thousand minutes.

I thought this was supposed to feel like unburdening. Instead, it feels like I am a tattletale, throwing Dad's saint of a mom under the bus. I am an accidental secret keeper who can't keep a secret.

What will this do to his view of her? I know it doesn't change my view of her, in fact the compassion I feel for my late grandmother has only grown. Pieces of her life now illuminated in my mind, complex but more humanizing than ever. Maybe I always knew there was something else. Maybe that's why I painted those paintings for my senior exhibition.

Even this doesn't define her, but it's a reminder that she's always been more than a short, quirky grandma who gave out cough drops and collected trinkets. She had an entire life of experiences. I only wish she had taken an opportunity to unload her secret while she was alive, so she didn't have to carry it alone. Knowing her, she did it out of protection for her kids and her family. I also can't help but think of Evelyn the little girl, the woman—there was probably a good helping of guilt, shame, and then punishing herself for years and years. But I'll never be able to know for sure.

I continue cautiously, affirming my mom's conclusion, and backing it up with a couple more sources. Dad is quiet. He stares down at those postcards and centimorgan charts and I can't even tell what he may be thinking.

His mind rewinding back before Pete. Before the move to Shelby, before the ulcers, and back to the tinny music box chimes of "The Waves of the Danube" ringing out in the night.

Processing silently over my Pandora's box of a binder, I wonder if he is frustrated—wracking his brain to remember the Eckstroms. Leon had moved Wilma and the younger girls down to Columbus around the fall of 1961. The Lawrentzes and the Eckstroms would never again cross paths. Dad didn't *get* a chance to remember them. He would've turned two at the end of that year.

Now he's 57 listening to his 33-year-old daughter describe to him the years he doesn't recall of his 33-year-old mother parting ways with the family who would forever be secretly connected to them all.

CHAPTER 15

ANALOG

May, 2017

"Therefore judge nothing before the appointed time; wait until
the Lord comes. He will bring to light what is hidden in darkness
and will expose the motives of the heart."
1 Corinthians 4:5

$\mathcal{A}$ while back, I had been watching an old home movie from 1989 of my 5th birthday. My parents, both sets of grandparents, little sister Samantha, my aunt, uncle, and baby cousin were in our home on West Main Street. Grandpa Scroggs, with his giant video camera hoisted on his right shoulder, filmed as I opened presents with the "help" of an 18-month-old Sammie. I looked up from my half-opened gift—a Barbie doll—and said, slowly and in child-like wonder, "Dad, it feels like...we're in...some kind of plaything...and we're just talking to everybody..." He cuts in as if to finish my thought. "It's like a dream, isn't it? You're just dreaming you're a Lawrentz!"

Things get cloudy when it comes to families and knowing the truth about where they came from. Especially when you have jokers and jesters in your family. What's meant to amuse can, at times, place a trinket-sized piece of doubt in a child's mind about their origins or the origins of those around them. An adult's own suspected adoption: "... there's no way I'm related to you people!" or teasing a child with: "We just found you in a field one day and thought we should take you home." The classic: "You must be the milk man's kid!" (In my family it was the "ice man".) Or the common Native American heritage lore: "Your great-great-great grandfather married a full-blooded Cherokee woman!"

Like a game of Family History Telephone, a generations-old truth can evolve into a story that has mingled with completely fabricated narratives resulting in the familial mythology we know and love today. We may not think much of its veracity when we first heard the tales and—unless you are the intensely curious sort or a habitual cynic—never think to doubt what you were told.

While there was one branch from my family that claimed Native heritage, my dad would tell us three girls we had royal blood. We were actual princesses and I fully believed it. To him, that was also the truth. His three little girls were *his* princesses.

My dad also liked to tease us with the stories of how he had two other families. He traveled to Michigan for work so often that he explained to us it was because his other wife Laura and children lived there. And when he had to go overseas to England it was to see Emma and his British kids there. We would roll our eyes and laugh and say, "Daa-aad!"

When he was away, he'd call to check in with my mom and she'd put us on the phone to say hi and tell him about our day. Occasionally he'd "talk to them," acting like they were right there in the room with him. We never believed him, but he has always been good at improv and maintaining a straight face when it suits him.

One time he took the joke too far. He talked about one of the families for too long. I knew they were made up, but he was so insistent about some incident he concocted being real and after a few minutes didn't break character like he usually did. The natural timing of the joke had come to an end. I felt my insides tighten and hot tears brimmed over the edge of my eyes. Something jealous and protective welled up in me. He was *my* dad, and he didn't belong to any other family. If he loved other wives and other children, it felt like that would mean who *I* was would change along with my place in his life. I did not like how that felt one bit.

Linda Ronstadt covered the Elvis Costello song, "Alison," and boy did Dad love Linda. He added another "L" and named me Allison Rae. I don't know how much my parents looked into what it meant, so much as choosing it because of the song and it being a popular name in the 1980's.

In 1984, it was only #51 on the Top 100 list for the country, but in our small-town, my graduating class included three Allisons. Initially, they were hoping for a boy to name Michael Jr. If it's a girl, maybe Michaela would suit, they thought.

While I couldn't remember back to age two like my dad, one of my first memories was from about age four when I was accused of using my mother's lotion. I don't know if they didn't want me using it at all, if it went missing, if too much was used, or what exactly the problem was—but in my memory I hadn't used it and said so. My dad insisted I had. Yet deep down I knew I wasn't lying. I was sitting on top of the washer in the basement during the experience for some reason. Had they put me up there? Surely I didn't climb up there on my own. Did the lotion have something to do with the laundry?

I recall the feeling of not being believed in that moment and it was one of those feelings I would experience in other situations over the years. The helplessness in not being able to change someone's mind or defend what you know is true, and even worse, the second guessing of your own experience. Feeling guilt and shame for things I wasn't guilty of. What if I *had* taken it? Used it and lied about it. Could I trust myself? Was I a liar? How could anyone trust my word if I couldn't believe myself?

Now as an adult, I think, what's the big deal? I accuse my kids of things occasionally and have given them enough fodder to see a therapist one day, I'm sure. The big deal, though, is if something sticks with you over time, keeps reappearing in various forms, it may deserve your attention. Other moments throughout my life caused me to second guess what I knew to be true and had me wondering if I really was a liar. Those feelings hadn't bubbled up for a long time, yet this specific situation found its way to my grown-up mind one evening in the midst of all this recent discovery.

Awake, but in dream-like thought, I brought the memory into my prayer time with Jesus. I asked if He had something to say about it. Was there something I needed to know or discover about that moment? Could He help me move past it for good? I saw myself as a four-year old again, sitting on that washer, unable to get down or get away from self-doubt and accusations. But things played out differently this time. Instead of my dad, Jesus stood in front of me. He called me by my name and told me He knew I was telling the truth. That I was a truth teller. All my surroundings collapsed into nothingness and suddenly I was sitting on top of the roof of my childhood home right next to Jesus. I could see everything from up there. Even at that height I felt safe and secure with Him there. Reassurance, peace, and truth filled in the cracks of that memory. It was such a realistic vision that I wept for the better part of the evening. It was a cleansing cry.

I took back some pieces of myself: a curious, intuitive, empathic person seeking out authenticity and truth. Like permission to believe in my own experience and memory even if it's not quite the perspective of someone else who was there.

A few days after my moment of clarity about truth and lies, I was going through a storage container (shocking, I know) and stumbled upon a familiar piece of my childhood. I had nearly forgotten all about it, but when I saw it, I instantly remembered the small wooden wall decoration that used to be in my room growing up. On the front was a glued-on cream colored paper background with black lettering. It read:

"Allison ~ Truthful One"

It was my dad who had given me this name. How fitting that the daughter of a man born of a long-held secret would struggle with wondering if she could trust her own thoughts and feelings as the truth while wondering if anyone else would ever believe the things she said. I couldn't help but wonder if that unseen force—something dark—was trying to keep me silent and unsure of myself so not only would I give up learning the truth, but that I also wouldn't have the courage to ever speak it out. It would get to work on me young, while I was moldable and vulnerable. Then I wouldn't be the truth-teller Jesus called me to be, I wouldn't go on to shine a light on this newfound truth to the person who needed to hear it the most: my dad. All along the plan had been to bury it.

I wondered if Grandma had felt that way. Like no one would believe her story if she decided to speak up. Like they would jump to conclusions and not understand. She may have even struggled to believe her own story. Even if her reality was to not let anyone know, she would keep evidence, keep souvenirs of her life. She kept a record.

During that moment on the video of my 5th birthday, my grandma was sitting on the living room couch, mostly out of the camera's view, watching me open presents when my dad said that line, "You're just dreaming you're a Lawrentz!" Off camera, you can hear my mom explain to everyone how I've been "saying things like 'I'm just dreaming it's my birthday' or something like that..." The joke about my dreaming about this or that (or being a Lawrentz) must have started around the time of this video and lasted into my teenage years, because it's something our family referred to all the time; it was one of our inside jokes. "I feel like I'm just dreaming I'm a Lawrentz!" we'd randomly exclaim for a laugh.

When I first said it as a child it was as if I was trying to figure out why I had been put in this particular family, in this certain time in history, and this place in the world. I was trying to understand a concept that was way too big of an idea for my young mind to comprehend: to understand my identity. To understand who we *all* were.

What if I knew the truth all along? Oddly enough, I *had* just been dreaming I was a Lawrentz. And now I'm wide awake.

Yes, feverishly wide awake and currently sitting across from my father at our old family dinner table—waiting for his response to the identity-altering news I just set before him. I hold my breath.

"I can shed Phil," he says resolutely, not breaking his gaze on the binder. He raises his head and looks across the table at no one. "I was named after him and he wasn't even my father..." he says with a little amusement in his voice. This person who was known to him as his genetic father, but who had not earned the title of Dad now wasn't either of those roles in his life.

Though legally he is Phillip Michael Lawrentz, two of those are names he doesn't have to emotionally own anymore. He always went by Michael or Mike. I think my grandma picked his name herself. I remembered seeing her in the 1946 Springfield Township yearbook with the nickname "Mike" printed beside her senior picture for some reason.

For 57 years, Dad wrestled with the idea of not only being the son of an abusive parent but being named after him. A person who hurt him and his siblings. Who abused their mom. Someone who made them all so afraid that as a little boy, Dad had stayed after school all alone in the building, hiding in a bathroom stall because a well-meaning but ignorant teacher had allowed Phil in to pick him up and take him home. He hid there until Phil left and then walked home alone.

I imagine his mind is doing what mine did weeks before as the revelation transfered from the physical evidence to my brain. My perspective of our family history screeched to a halt, like stopping a VHS as it fast forwards and pressing the rewind button twice to make it fly back to the beginning. Only now, all the scenes you knew by heart on the well-worn tape were replaced by ones you never saw before. There were still scenes that seemed familiar enough; they were just all shot at an angle that changed your whole perspective of the story.

Standing in school lines with other last names starting with E, surrounded by D's and F's instead of K's and M's. There were also new people at family gatherings, birthday parties with new people to celebrate with, more weddings to attend. Growing up with the same extended family but the addition of an entire new branch. *How would we have changed each other's lives had we been aware of each other's existence? What did we get deprived of? Or what were we saved from?* An exciting unease had filled my body as I tried to make sense of it all. Learning this made me different somehow. *Everything* was different.

"I guess nothing surprises me anymore at my age," he continues. "How wild!" I don't have to do any convincing. He accepts it. Both he and Mom understand how I got to this conclusion—and it makes sense to them.

I can tell questions are starting to form.

"I wonder," he begins slowly, "maybe you could ask Jen, whenever you talk to her next, about his height? Or maybe the sisters know…I'm just wondering how tall Leon was."

"Sure, Dad. I'll ask her."

Feeling more at ease, I also show him the two postcards to get his thoughts about which "Leon" Grandma might be referring to.

As we make light of some heavy things, the weight is melting off my shoulders. Dad isn't disappointed in me; he isn't angry. He doesn't accuse me of tarnishing his mom's good name. He doesn't think I'm lying. I told him the truth, and he believed me.

The last couple of months I walked around doing normal errands feeling sick with responsibility. Paranoia and anxiety. As if history had a mafia-mentality and would do whatever it took to make sure I kept my mouth shut about something I should have never witnessed or dug up. I wore sunglasses and ball caps and walked briskly through stores, heart pounding as I grabbed a box of dry pasta, a bag of baby carrots, the jug of milk. *Dredging up the past never did anyone any good. Oh, why didn't you just mind your own business?*

But all that paranoia and anxiety fell away during this time with my dad. The secret wants you to feel shame and regret. It accuses. When it's brought into the light, its name changes. It's no longer a *secret*. It's a *truth*.

In my imagination, I time travel to late 1958. Before I existed and before my dad existed. On East Walnut Street, the Lawrentz family decides they should invest in new aluminum siding for their small white house—perhaps they are approached by an eager salesman about their need for such a remodel. Phil signs a paper for the contractors to start their work—I highly doubt Evelyn has any say in the matter.

But now, in 2017, I can see the progress taking place within the pictures Grandma took of her kids in their backyard and on the porch over the course of fall/winter 1958 to winter/spring 1959. There are even pictures where she stood across the street to capture the whole house transformation. The addition of new siding and the enclosure of their porch, covering over the wooden spindles and railings. The window trim in this picture changed to white while previously it had been black. A second back door was now covered entirely by siding. The origins of this life-changing story were hidden in images I'd seen so many times before.

I leave my parents' house. I think I may be able to sleep well for the first time in a while. But maybe not, since now my mind is racing from the rush of having told Dad.

"I think I'd confront Mom about it if she were still here," he had said. "I think she'd own up to it." There were questions Jen and the sisters just couldn't answer. These questions were for his mom.

Evelyn had plenty of reasons not to tell anyone, and it's doubtful we'll ever know exactly why. Maybe she convinced herself she was having Phil's child. Name him Phillip Michael. Ignore the red hair and obvious resemblance to Leon and his daughters. Move on with life. Survive.

Denial of the truth can be very powerful. You bury it deep enough to rewrite the reality of your experience.

But I wrestle with a nagging thought. You'd think someone who wanted to keep something hidden would destroy every trace and hint of the past. Or at least attempt to. But if you're a record keeper, you'd find a loophole so you don't have to destroy anything. You hide them in plain sight in order to keep pieces of the past.

I log onto *Ancestry.com* and click the tab to find my tree and I start deleting.

The Mumaws and the Clarks. *Delete.* The Burgesses and Allmans—gone. The Lawrentz'. I pause. I'm surprised by the twinge of grief I feel at the impending click of the *Delete* button. On each click, Ancestry asks me the same question: *Are you sure you want to permanently delete this person from your tree?*

An imaginary identity was built based on our surname. Traditionally your father's side of the family determines your last name. From your father's, his father's, and his father's father. It's stripped down to the sacred paternal memento people seek out at heritage festivals and medieval fairs where you can have crests or coats of arms made—printed and framed to be "heraldry-as-wall-art" for showing the grandkids. A proud conversation piece for friends and neighbors during a visit.

My dad had gone from Phillip Michael Lawrentz to Phillip Michael Eckstrom (in the genetic sense). He had gone by his step-dad Pete's last name, Boreman, for a period of time in high school, but it never became legal. "Now what names do I include on my headstone someday?" he mused. P. Michael Lawrentz Boreman Eckstrom. And in what order? Order of knowledge or order when they came into his life.

Delete.

Everyone else is in bed, and I'm in the living room with only the light from my laptop screen. *I just deleted a quarter of my family tree.* I think about the Lawrentz family members I have relationships with—the family I grew up with, those whom I dearly love. We still belong to each other, though I know each of them will process this news in their own way when they inevitably hear about it.

Telling my dad tonight was like getting permission to delete the branch from our tree. For whatever reason, the act of physically deleting it makes everything feel so real and now I can bring myself to do it.

Pedigree view.

Phillip Michael Lawrentz, 1959-Living. A thin line branches to the upper right of his name in the space that had occupied Phil Lawrentz' name. I click the box with the prompt + *Add father* and carefully enter information in each field.

First and Middle Name: *Leon Gustav*

Last Name: *Eckstrom*

Birth Date: *7 Feb 1923*

Birthplace: *Davenport, Iowa*

Death Date: *12 Mar 1999*

Death Place: *Akron, Ohio*

I click the button.

Save.

PART III

PART III

CHAPTER 16

PENMANSHIP

May, 2017

"Life is infinitely stranger than anything which the mind of man could invent. We would not dare to conceive the things which are really mere commonplaces of existence. If we could fly out of that window hand in hand, hover over this great city, gently remove the roofs, and peep in at the queer things which are going on, the strange coincidences, the plannings, the cross-purposes, the wonderful chains of events, working through generations, and leading to the most outré results, it would make all fiction with its conventionalities and foreseen conclusions most stale and unprofitable."[3]

I want to find out all I can about Leon. After all, he is now (and of course always has been) my grandfather.

Our monthly budget not only includes electricity, groceries, Netflix, piano lessons for Clementine, summer baseball for Miles, but I also have a genealogy budget. I would gladly say goodbye to TV and JIF peanut butter if I had to choose between those and getting rid of my record-hunting addiction.

---

[3]Arthur Conan Doyle, *The Complete Adventures of Sherlock Holmes* (New York: Harper & Brothers, 1892; Project Gutenberg, May 20, 2019), www.gutenberg.org/ebooks/1661.

Records on both *Ancestry.com* and *Newspapers.com* provide a stream of mentions about Leon, and I want to take some time to go through each one. They span from the 1930s through the early 1970s.

First, it's the school, social events, contests, and music related mentions, then come birth announcements ("the proud father of [another] baby girl!"), ads for places he worked, and legal notices or arrests that appeared in ink within the *Mansfield News Journal*. I know I need to make a trip to the Mansfield Courthouse at some point, but I continue my late-night online searches to exhaust the digital trail until I can get there in person.

I ask Jen about a Social Security Application file I find for him on Ancestry's database. Listed as Leon Gustav Eckstrom in 1937, 1988, and 1991. Another name on his file, with no date beside it, lists him as Richard L. Edwards. Jen hasn't heard that name before and tells me it is either an error or it could be one of his aliases. I make a note to dig into that later.

The first newspaper ad I see with his name on it is a 1948 ad for Zephyr Awnings in Mansfield. There is a John Chahulski listed as Manager of Installation along with Leon as an engineer and Manager of Sales.

Next was a legal notice in May 1949. Wilma had filed for divorce and wanted custody of their three girls on grounds of neglect and cruelty. Obviously, something stopped the divorce proceedings because they wouldn't legally divorce until 1968.

On July 22, 1957, there's a short article in the *Mansfield News Journal*: "Mr. and Mrs. Carl Eckstrom, 440 Pearl Avenue, and Mr. and Mrs. Leon Eckstrom, 256 Ruth Avenue, returned from a trip to Davenport, Iowa; Chicago; and Galesburg, Illinois. They had attended funeral services for Carl's brother Siegfried Eckstrom. They also visited Mrs. Carl Eckstrom's mother [Selma Johnson Magnus] in Davenport and her son [Carl Jr.] in Chicago."

Never keeping one job too long, Leon stayed in the sales, contracting, and engineering realm. While on the ethics and integrity front, he may have been questionable (so I hear), intelligence was not something he seemed to lack. By 1958, he had sinced moved on from the awning company. Between general contracting, auto sales, drinking too much whiskey, chasing women, parking violations, betting on horse races, and instructing bookies, he was able to land a sales position at the Mansfield Siding Company.

The ad from December 31, 1958, shows images of Leon and seven other men who worked there with the header *"Your family should know our family! Come in and meet them at Mansfield Siding Company, 63 South Diamond Street, Mansfield."*

Based on those pictures my grandma took outside their home on Walnut Street in early 1959, I had noted the significant difference to their porch and the back of their house—it was clear that some new siding had been put up and a porch enclosure built. Linda Eckstrom had told Jen she thought that Leon had sold the Lawrentz family siding and that's how she thinks the two families first met. The timing seemed to be confirmation of her memory. I would love to have physical proof in the form of a contract or receipt of service with dates, an address, and both Phil and Leon's names on it. I am so spoiled and greedy. But between Grandma's pictures, the newspaper ad date, Linda's story, and my dad's birthdate, enough things added up for me.

Next, a series of articles about a forgery from 1959 catches my eye within the list of results. I read them carefully, making sure I absorb every detail and file them away in my mind, ready to pull them back out when new information and clues inevitably surface.

The first of these is from October 31, 1959, in the *Mansfield News Journal.*

"Held by Sheriff—Bucyrus police yesterday turned Mansfielder Leon Eckstrom, 38, of 1594 Wooster Road over to Richland County Sheriff's deputies who are now holding him on a non-support warrant and investigation of possible forgery charges."

Looks like the "Best Penmanship" skills of his youth paid off. The article continues: *"Deputy Gibb Moore said Eckstrom had an infected bullet wound in his leg when he arrived here and said the man explained he had been shot accidentally."* Accidentally—by whom? Himself or someone else?

"Deputy Moore said the man's apartment was searched and a small duffle bag was found which contained two revolvers, a blonde wig, two boxes of ammunition, screwdrivers, wire cutters, and other tools."

I reread that part. What an oddly specific list of things to find in a general contractor's work bag. Three items in that list seem reasonable... and three do not. Of course "other tools" may fit in both categories, depending.

"Eckstrom was admitted to Mansfield General Hospital for treatment of the gunshot wound in his leg. Meanwhile deputies are investigating the man's past actions and what use, if any, the items in the duffel bag might have been put."

The next article mentioning the case was on November 5th.

"Held For Action By Grand Jury: 2 Charged With Forgery—A Mansfield man and woman were bound to the Richland County grand jury on forgery charges today... Mrs. Frances L. McDonald of 138 Grasmere Ave., and Leon Gustavson Eckstrom, 38, of 1594 Wooster Rd., entered innocent pleas to charges of forging a check in the amount of $135. Each was bound over under $2,500 bond."

Frances McDonald. Must be the blonde wig. I wonder if she was another lady-friend, a business partner, or an unwilling party?

The article continues and gives a recap of the October 31st article.

"HAD LEG INFECTION—Eckstrom was turned over to sheriff's deputies on Oct. 30 on a non-support warrant. When arrested he was found to be in possession of two revolvers, ammunition, wire cutters, screwdrivers, and other tools."

They left out the wig!

"Deputies said Eckstrom had a leg infection which he said was a result of an accidental bullet wound. Mrs. McDonald was arrested in connection with the Eckstrom case. (Sic.)"

And while Leon was sitting in jail awaiting trial, Wilma gave birth to their youngest daughter, Karen, on December 19th, and of course Evelyn had given birth to my dad the day before.

A *"son [was born] to Mr. and Mrs. Phillip Lawrentz, 315 East Walnut St."* as recorded in the *Ashland Times Gazette.* It was also listed in the *Mansfield News Journal* under a number of Ashland Births on page 12 in the December 26, 1959 edition. In this same newspaper, three pages back, Leon's forgery charge is mentioned in a list of "25 Criminal Cases"—case transcripts that were filed in the county clerk's office for the upcoming jury session.

His first plea was entered: *Innocent.* By February 8, 1960, he had changed his plea to guilty and paid back the money from the bad checks. The notice reads, *"Gets 5-Year Probation: Leon G. Eckstrom, 38, of 1159 Wooster Road pleaded guilty to a forgery indictment today and was placed on probation for five years by Judge James J. Mayer. Eckstrom's attorney told the court that restitution for bad checks had been made."*

There was no more detail about their looking into his *"past actions and what use, if any, the items in the duffel bag might have been put"* as the paper had said back on October 31st.

###

It's nearing the end of May. I read a new message from Jen: "It has been so interesting working through this journey of investigation with you. I love that we both happen to be interested in genealogy enough to get on Ancestry and were able to meet each other. I've also learned a lot more about my mom's memories of her dad as a result of conversations about this, which I really appreciate."

I ask her if she'd like to meet up sometime in person. We look at our calendars to find a date that will work. I take a deep breath to calm the feeling of butterflies and nervousness that grabs me at the thought of a meeting. We set a date for the end of June, and I wonder what her voice will sound like.

I had finally carved out some time to explore the courthouse for more records. This time I'm driving the twenty minutes southwest; I go past signs for Lahm Airport, then over the railroad tracks that sit in the shadow of the grain silos. Large, red letters painted on the silos read: *Welcome to Mansfield*. Almost immediately after my welcome, I pass Dad's old office. Glancing at my phone, the Google Maps blue line says I'm almost to my first destination.

I want to look at a couple of Leon's old workplaces while I am here so I pull over into a nearby parking lot and survey the old brick building with doors he must have gone in and out of. They had seen better days: maybe they were completely vacant now, aside from the gaunt old man who sat in the doorway of one entrance, smiling for my camera. I take just a couple of pictures on my phone to examine later and make my way to the middle of town.

Finding a parking spot on the street right out in front of the courthouse, I place a few quarters in the parking meter and hustle down the walkway trying to beat the sprinkle of rain tapping on my shoulder. Passing under the tall white arches that frame the front of the courthouse I duck inside, trying my best to look like I know where to go. Glancing quickly at the signs after passing through a two-manned metal detector, I make my way to the Clerk of Courts office. I notice it's a bit busier than Ashland's office was when I was searching for divorce records. After just a few moments, I am next in line.

A short, thin woman with permed mousy-brown hair, ripe with Aqua-Net, looks up at me from her folder filing in the center of the room. "Can I help you?"

"Yes, I'm looking for some criminal trial records from 1960." Putting down her folder, she opens and walks through the hinged countertop, waving me on to follow her down a hallway off the main office area.

"1960?" I nod. "Okay, come on with me, we'll getcha set up on a microfiche machine. Have you used one of those before?"

"Yes, just a couple times."

"What's the name of the person you're looking for? Do you have a specific date in 1960?" I give her the information as she finds and opens a large book of records for the letter E.

"Ecker, Eckstein, Eck—Eckstrom, Leon. Here it is." She mumbles and repeats the canister number to herself, and I just observe, helpless and following her while crossing over to the metal cabinet full of records—shrunken images tightly wound up on film. She taps two fingers as if they were stepping on each white box moving deeper to the back of the cabinet.

"And we have a winner," she joked, pulling the correct small box from its place and simultaneously moving forward to a machine. She makes sure I am settled in front of it and am able to start scanning the files before flitting back down the hall, back to her folder filing duties. "Let me know if you get stuck!"

Once again, I'm back at another velociraptor sounding machine with a dial as touchy as the accelerator of an amusement park bumper car. One careless turn to the right and *zing!* Warp speed. I figure slower is better even if it takes me longer. All the noisy dials make me anxious. But there's no rush; I'll just hum along at a consistent pace but not so fast that I can't read the dates and names that move along the screen. The whirring of my scanning slows to a crawl; I squint to concentrate even more and soon I stop altogether—there he is. Case number 6093.

The documents are so dark, and most words are barely legible. Pages that detail a warrant for his arrest and the records of bad checks he made can be examined at home. Hopefully I can make out most of the print outs. *Push green to print.*

Green. Green. Green. Green.

Green.

Home with my freshly printed pieces of the past, I learn that Walter Wixon, an accountant, as well as the vice-president and treasurer of T&A Saveway in Mansfield, was the witness that set these charges in motion.

First, with the Affidavit Charging Offense document and then a non-support warrant for Leon's arrest on November 4th. He and Wilma were still married at this time, but he was supposed to be helping her with the rent and feeding his kids.

I read on. The first check he made is for September 8, 1959. He attempted to cash it at the Farmers Savings and Trust Company in Mansfield, paid to the order of T&A Saveway for $200. Leon signs the check as "Robert J. Fox".

Remembering a 1957 *Mansfield News Journal* article, I know Frances McDonald worked at T&A Saveway and served as a "clerk's seat second vice-president" for a term that year. I wonder about Walter Wixon—did he know Frances from the store?

The second check is dated five days later September 13, 1959. This time the signature was a woman's: Elsie Dildomedes. If I were a gamblin' gal I'd say "Elsie" was Frances McDonald in a blonde wig with an unfortunate stage name. But, of course, I can't say for certain. The bank he (or they) visited on this particular stop was The First National Bank of Ashland (now razed), with its motto "the Oldest Bank of Ashland Since 1852," and the check made out to "cash" in the amount of $135.

The Ashland Bank and Savings Company (which still stands on Main Street) was the location for his last forgery attempt. This check was dated the very next day, September 14, 1959, and also made out to "cash"—this time for $145 and signed by "Richard Dilgard." In the memo line of the check was a note about Safety Deposit Boxes For Rent.

These small amounts seem a little petty to me. But it was 1959. Curious, I plug in the numbers and the year on Google. In 2017's money, the amounts listed on the checks range from $1200-$1800. A worthwhile price for the trouble, I suppose.

The report continues. On January 15, 1960, Leon and his parents Carl and Helen make a court appearance to acknowledge that they would owe the state of Ohio the sum of $2,500 (over $20,000 in today's money) if Leon failed to personally appear before the court of common pleas on the first day of the trial. And if they couldn't pay, the court could legally take their house. They could take everything.

All three of them signed this document. Carl. Helen. Leon. Did Carl and Helen support Leon because he was their son, or because they had grandchildren who needed a father to provide for them? Maybe they had hoped that he could eventually get his act together if he got this second chance.

Honestly, I don't know if it was a second chance or a twenty-second. I glance at my binder of other info nearby, where I put a copy of my great-grandfather's obituary. Carl passed away twenty years later in 1980, and no mention was even made of Leon. "He is survived by his wife Helen M. Magnus Eckstrom; one son, Carl B. of Cleveland; one daughter, Helen..."

One son.

I suspect this whole forgery business wasn't the first or only thing that damaged their relationship.

Case No. 6093: The Court of Common Pleas and the State of Ohio, plaintiff vs. Leon Eckstrom, defendant.

Robert E. Mabee became his appointed attorney and must have counseled Leon to withdraw his former plea of not guilty and to enter a plea of guilty to the indictment now on two counts, instead of four. The great compromise. The court agreed to the motion. There was talk of probation and no jail time as a possible sentence.

"On February 8, 1960, came the prosecuting attorney and represented to the court that the January 1960 term of Richland County grand jury had returned a sub rosa indictment upon four counts charging defendant with forgery and an open court for good cause shown leave was requested for an order of nolle prosequi. To said sub rosa indictment and upon consideration it is ordered adjudged and decreed that the said sub rosa indictment to be removed from the depository."

The next journal entry showed how charming and persuasive people have said Leon could be.

"On February 8, 1960, defendant being in court represented by his attorney, Robert Mabee for further proceedings upon indictment charging him with forgery to counts to which indictment defendant entered his plea of guilty... and it appearing to the court that the character of the

*defendant and the circumstances of the case are such that he is not likely
to again engage in an offensive course of conduct and that the public good
does not demand or require that the defendant Leon Gustav Eckstrom
be immediately sentenced."*

He was then placed on probation for five years.

Terms of the Probation:

*"February 8th 1960 to the probation officer of Richland County Ohio
on the following terms and conditions: That he is not to partake in any
intoxicating beverage or to visit or frequent any place where intoxicating
beverages are sold; that he refrain from all law violations. That he avoid
the company of all improper companions of both sexes; that he refrain
from gambling or visiting gambling places or other improper places of
amusement; that he immediately seek employment and remain employed
if possible; that he shall not change his residence from Richland County,
Ohio without the express permission of the probation officer of Richland
County, Ohio; that he shall be of good conduct generally; that he shall
pay all lawful obligations; that he shall keep an itemized statement of
the amount of his earnings and expenditures each and every month.
That he shall make monthly reports to said probation officer...*

*Signed Judge J. Mayer, Prosecuting attorney Theodore Lutz, and the
attorney for the defendant Robert Mabee."*

He also had a 10 PM curfew.

As for Frances, the *News Journal* mentions her in the hospital releases for
February 17, 1960. Not sure when or why she was admitted. Elsewhere (in
the same paper) it shows all charges against her were dropped.

The Eckstrom family had permission to move to Columbus near the end
of 1961, and Leon took a job with North American Rockwell as an engineer.
Mansfield was now in their rear-view mirror, and they had no reason to visit
Ashland ever again. February 8, 1965, Leon was released from his probation
terms and was "restored to full rights of citizenship." A free man. A man
not likely to "engage in an offensive course of conduct" ever again.

Fall, 2016

Standing on gravel and shattered glass that, up until a few minutes prior, was a fully intact car window. I looked over at the sign in front of our little white Ford Escape. "A safe and fun place for the whole family." The sun beat down, but it finally felt like autumn sun, not like the scorching heat of summer. The perfect day for a walk.

"Why don't you all take the kids back to the house—Allison and I will wait for the police," Jason said to his parents. They were in town visiting from Virginia for his birthday, and we decided to take them to a local park just down the road from our home. Every July, thousands of people gather here to see the hot air balloon festival; one of our small town's trademark events (other than the annual County Fair). But it was September and the big crowds and balloons were gone; just the occasional cyclist or family out using this idyllic public park trail.

When we found out our car had been broken into, we immediately reached the local police and then called to have our bank accounts frozen. We did what we could to prevent the thief from using any of our debit and credit cards, checkbook, or my driver's license. In the time it took for us to walk the short, paved loop through the woods and around the field, someone had shattered the window, grabbed my purse and i-Phone, and took off. The bank assured us we'd done the right thing by calling them and the authorities. And that they'd take care of everything.

I looked around for any clues to what could have happened but nothing obvious stood out. A jogger I recognized from the trail earlier was making another loop.

"Excuse me," I shouted, interrupting his pace. I quickly filled him in on the incident. "We wondered if you happened to see another vehicle here. Or anything strange if you were on the loop earlier?"

"Uh—oh, wow!" He jogged to a stop to see the smashed-in window for himself. "No, I'm sorry, I didn't! On the last loop I remember seeing your vehicle and the window was *definitely not* broken—I would have noticed it shattered like that. I didn't see another vehicle here besides that mini-van over there." He pointed toward the part of the lot nearest the barn.

The vehicle seemed to belong to a small family getting pictures taken by the large white barn in the field. I wondered if they saw anything. My face felt hot as I walked across the gravel lot and through the grass to interrupt their session. To my disappointment, they hadn't either.

The two children, about my kids' ages, were busy kicking at the pieces of gravel in the lawn. "I wonder if it happened when we were taking pictures on the other side of the barn?" their mother offered. I thanked her anyway but inside I turned away completely annoyed. How could you have not heard or seen *anything*?

✿

May, 2017

The recollection of that day eight months prior came to my mind as I connected the incident to an echo of the past—as if Leon had been involved in stealing my identity and committed theft and forgery from the grave to somehow get my attention for what was soon to be discovered. Or maybe this was what was meant by paying for the sins of the father.

What followed was bounced checks, late fees, and a stolen identity. As if on a machine loop, real live people working at the bank kept with the script no matter what question I threw at them. "I'm sorry, there's nothing we can do. An investigation is pending." I thought about all the time I spent wrapped up in phone calls, being placed on hold, writing emails, making personal visits to the bank, and being told the manager wasn't available. Convenient. It felt like *we* were the ones being investigated. Paying the price for a crime we didn't commit.

Between the police officer on the case and other bank branch managers who *would* talk to me at first, I discovered the thief stole someone else's checkbook from a different park and began making checks out to "Allison Barnhart" for various amounts of money. They were able to cash these forged checks automatically at the other branches even though the bank had assured us we'd taken all the proper steps to prevent ID theft. As an extra measure, they had added a special alert to our account so ID fraud would not be possible. And yet it happened. Repeatedly.

The continuing investigation meant freezing the only account that we had money in. Any income through our direct deposit was frozen and we weren't allowed to have access to it. I had to go in and cash out our kids' savings accounts to get grocery money. My parents helped us pay bills that came due.

We soon learned the "alert" on our account that was used to prevent the thief from using my ID and committing forgery was never actually activated. The police sent two subpoenas to get video footage at the branches where the suspect showed up; the banks reported that the footage had "probably been destroyed by now." The process of signing an affidavit upfront and connecting me to their corporate offices—what they should have done in the first place was done too late.

Apparently, my doppelgänger had been running amok. The police officer on our case had said how one of the bank tellers reported that a thirty-something red-headed woman had been seen going through the drive-thru.

"They said she looked just like you!" Well, why don't we just go get her a DNA kit and see if there's a relation there.

After three or four successful deceptions at various branches, she got spooked and left my ID and debit card behind in the suction tube container.

But back on the day of the break in, I had gathered some of the car window glass that shattered and went all over the gravel lot and inside our white Ford Escape. I took the pieces of pretty teal glass out from my jeans pocket they were shoved in and put them into a tiny clear container. A strange souvenir of a stressful moment that quickly turned into a few stress-filled months.

Something my grandma might think to save, no doubt.

CHAPTER 17

MAKE THE WORLD GO AWAY
May, 2017

In a black sheath dress stands a young Evelyn, glancing toward the floor. She wears her short dark hair full of curls half-pinned in a side part, revealing one of a pair of elegant dangling pearl earrings. Her unpinned hair covers half of her forehead and right eye in a glamorous way. Her arms are folded in front of her so that her right-hand peeks out and displays cherry-red fingernails which catch the light and glisten as if they are still drying.

Quietly she continues looking down, maybe at her Lifestride pumps, maybe the floor. It's hard to tell where we are. Not outdoors, no, some empty undecorated room with wooden panels and built-ins. She seems pensive and tired; I don't know what to say. I think she knows I'm here.

"Grandma?" I say to this young woman. Her attention moves from the ground to me. I'm full of curiosity and deep affection for her.

"Grandma...who is Leon?"

I want *her* to tell me. I want to know who he is to her. I want to tell her I know who he is to us now. She remains quiet and a calm smile appears on her face. Before she can answer I stir and am out of the dream.

I get the feeling if I were to stay with her longer, she wouldn't have told me anyway.

Dreams held meaning, and my dad and I paid attention to them. He'd share premonitions or dreams he had with me that in some respect came true. And I'd share mine with him. Grandma Boreman was no exception; she had her share of spooky incidents where a thought or dream of hers came to fruition.

Our "ESPN," Dad calls it. Then there are the dreams like this that don't seem to predict anything, but instead leave me in a state of limbo.

The question remains: *Who is my Uncle Frank's father?* The four hypotheses determined for him are:

1. He is another secret son of Leon's: Not impossible. But it would have to have been a long-term secret affair that continued even after the Eckstroms moved to Columbus.
2. He is Grandpa Boreman's son: Farfetched, but not ruling it out.
3. His father is a mystery someone: Also farfetched, but not impossible.
4. He was Phil's son: Probable and likely.

Only one way to start ruling things out. I open the email I've anticipated receiving from Ancestry, though I do so wincing a little. I click the "Your results are in!" button and scan the page for percentages and centimorgans. Shares only 1,780cMs with Dad. And only 3% Scandinavian. And just like that, I have proof my dad and his youngest brother are half-brothers.

It's already 9:30, the kids are in bed, and I should really wind down, too. But how can I sleep when I have this weighing over my head? Is it curiosity or duty that makes this kind of research seem so urgent? A wave of excitement yet a miserable and sobering responsibility sets in—an all too familiar feeling.

I search for Robin Lawrentz or any others who may match him as a Lawrentz descendant. Robin hadn't matched my dad but *should* match Frank. I will still have to wait for Uncle Jim's test results to make a full comparison with Frank and the rest of the Lawrentzes.

I click on Robin to compare with Frank: "...is either not a DNA match or has not taken a DNA test." I sink a little and close my eyes as if to reset the screen. Maybe another answer will appear when I reopen them.

Well, that didn't work. I cringe and begin to realize hypothesis No. 3 was most likely the answer. *Another mystery someone.*

I panic. With Father's Day approaching next month—what on earth am I going to tell three brothers who now have three completely different fathers from one another? It seems likely that Uncle Jim's father is actually Phil, but until I get his results back and compare them with Dad's and Frank's, I can't be certain of anything.

I should get some sleep. But first, I should call my parents. Maybe I'll be able to sleep after I get this new information off my chest.

They pick up after a couple of rings.

"Are you sitting down?" I ask. "You're not gonna believe this."

❧

It's morning and whatever sleep I got seems sufficient. I message the Ancestry member who is listed as administrator of the test with the highest amount of DNA that matches Uncle Frank (out of the matches I don't recognize as being maternal matches, of course). I confirm the match isn't also on my dad's list, so it's likely a paternal connection for Frank. It's a full first cousin match with no full name, only initials. This cousin, "E.K.," also has a private tree. Now it is up to them, whoever they are, to see the notification that they have a message from me.

I look at a few public trees of the mystery cousin's more distant matches; they show a few names from areas in Ohio, and even in our hometown. I'm on the right track, but how long will this part of the puzzle take to figure out? I try to be patient. I offload one closeted skeleton only to gain another. She collected stamps, dolls, rocks, and apparently life-altering family secrets as well.

❧

Four days have passed—Uncle Jim's results are finally here. I don't know if I can take another set of unexpected results. I breathe a sigh of relief. I see Lawrentz matches right away. Results I expected for my dad and for Frank. I check Frank's list again—just in case.

Not *one* Lawrentz.

It's not just a lack of Lawrentz relatives submitting DNA samples—I *know* they exist because of Jim's results. Isn't that pretty solid supporting evidence? None of the Lawrentz relations on his list show up on Mike and Frank's. And why should they? They had a different father than Jim!

Two NPEs. I make a note to mention this when I eventually sit down with all of them in person and explain everything. Was it "Non-Paternity Event"? Or "Not Parent Expected"? Experts in the field seem to use both. The former sounds more academic to me—I'll use that. And if I need to have another reason for my conclusion? Shared DNA amount. The centimorgan range between Jim and Frank is just as low as it is between Dad and both brothers. Another comparison: Dad and Susie also have a similar amount. They all fall into the half-sibling ranges shown in the chart.

I quickly look at the matches the brothers have in common. They stand right out as maternal matches—Grandma's relatives. Cousins from Georgia and surrounding areas that have surnames I recognize from the England and Bowers trees. At least I can tell them no, they aren't adopted, although they had joked and maybe half-hoped it would be true.

Back in my inbox, I see another unopened email for returned test results. My own test. The least of my concerns right now and a footnote in my mind, but here it is all the same. I open it like all the others and see both of my parents' names at the top of my matches list. I read it like a verdict from the jury.

I am the child of Melinda and P. Michael. Both my parents and I match all the people I expected us to match with, including my new Eckstrom relatives; the partial bloodline transfusion is complete.

I update my parents (my now co-conspirators and fellow secret keepers) and ask them to help arrange a time to have both of Dad's brothers over to their house so I can give them the news. Here we go again. But how will they react? Goodbye sleep. Goodbye nerves. At least for the next few weeks while I wait for judgment day.

And still, I'm compelled to keep searching—going over things again and again in hopes of even more understanding. I pick up a printed photo of my Aunt Linda dated September 1961 that I previously studied in the aftermath of yanking all totes and bins out of my basement a month or so ago. What new thing might this photo have to say?

An 11-year-old Linda Lawrentz is holding a small baby. Her gaze is straight into the camera. I flip it over. "Linda Lawrentz and Carol and Ray's baby" And in parentheses: "Vermillion."

Before, the names would have meant nothing to me. *Family friends I'd never heard of,* I would have thought. And Vermilion is a town north of us right on Lake Erie. Initially I guess I assumed they were at a fair in Vermilion. The double "l" in it hadn't crossed my mind before. *A simple misspelling, perhaps.*

"This is the Ashland County Fair," I whisper to no one.

It's in mid-September every year. I strain my eyes and dare the black and white photograph to give me more. I think it's safe to assume Evelyn took the picture. Where was Carol? Wilma, Leon, and the younger daughters had already moved to Columbus that summer. Why did *Grandma and Aunt Linda* have her baby with them at the fair?

With my mind now full of even more information, names, and dates, I continue to immerse myself in everything left behind I can get my hands on. All the lost and found things. They are little treasures and I handle each saved Valentine's card or cut-out postmark with care.

A pair of black Lifestride pumps in a shoebox are in my closet. They were hers, but I'm not sure when she wore them. I pretend they are from 1959. A playlist of hit songs from that year is on shuffle and loop through my Spotify account. I am in a trance of the 1950s and 60s.

I try to be present during the day when the kids are around. It's difficult. I think about how my grandma was once a mom my age watching her two little kids play outside in the summer; helping them get into swimsuits for the kiddie pool, making them snacks, breaking up sibling squabbles, and tending to scraped knees. And only two blocks up the street and two generations later, here I am doing the same.

My eyes drift to a cigar box full of negatives sitting in the next tote from the basement. I saw them years before and wondered why no one had ever tossed them out. Opening the lid with King Edward's face, the cigar smell is long gone. Now it's aged paper and chemical scented. The negatives varied in shape and size. Decades of picture taking stacked up in old paper sleeves. 127, 120, 620, 35mm. Sending in the stacks to be reprinted is probably an expensive idea.

Skipper!

I remember my mom had given me this old light box with Barbie's kid sister Skipper on it that was used to trace drawings. It's a child's light box, but it just might work. I slowly plug in the nasty looking two-prong cord end into the outlet, bracing myself for inevitable sparks and possible electrocution.

All good.

I place rows of negatives from the cigar box carefully on the light, take a picture of it with my phone and move on to the next set. This is taking a while. The smell of the heat makes me work quicker. The negatives are so hot they start to curl and bend, so I stop. I pull the plug out of the wall and let the whole contraption cool down.

It's a good start.

With my laptop, I upload the images of negatives, opening them in Photoshop.

Open.

Command+I.

One by one I invert them and I'm able to see clearly what is in each photo. I crop and adjust the contrast and levels if needed, save it out, and open the next one. My one-woman assembly line.

A camera was always within Grandma's reach, and she'd take it with her to most events. Encouraged by Mae's interest in photography, Evelyn too loved to document moments in her everyday world, and it became an essential part of her routine. She'd take her 12 exposures all at the same moment or over a span of days; have someone drive her to the photo lab downtown, walk, or send it out in the mail; and wait for the film to be processed and printed. Usually in doubles or triples.

I wonder whether she thought about being able to remember the past later in life or she simply wanted to capture what she saw in the present without much thought to the consequences.

Compared with the way I take pictures today, her way had to have been more intentional than the modern approach. Rarely ordering prints and having almost unlimited space on a device that serves as a camera and my phone creates a seriously flippant approach to photography. While I can say I might think through some of my shots, I take most of them for granted.

I recognize many from the prints I've seen in our family for years. It will take some time, but this seems like the best solution to check for any images that no longer have printed photos that accompany them. Maybe ones that Phil took from her and never returned; maybe ones Pete destroyed. Ones she cut herself or others out of. And, of course, ones that just got lost or ruined with the passage of time, not to mention living in over twenty different places. With that much moving around, I can't believe that any of this still exists.

I never knew Grandma to be musically inclined, but I learned she had taken piano lessons as a young girl. She never told me about it while she was alive. I think she loved listening to music more. The crooning of Peggy Lee, Eddy Arnold, and of course Elvis would sound from her record player. In particular, Dad remembered an Eddy Arnold song she would put on when she was feeling extra melancholy.

I had to admit I had never heard of it, so one evening I looked it up and listened. A clear voice rang out along with backup singers filling in with a repeated line of melody after Eddy's phrasing and then some "ahhs" that made you sway and feel his inner despair. A piano tickled the ivories the way it does on Patsy Cline songs.

"Do you remember when you loved me? / Before the world took me astray? / If you do then forgive me / And make the world go away."

I understood why she liked it.

A few months ago, in our *before* life, my dad bought a handful of tickets to a musical duo who were dubbed "the female version of The Everly Brothers." The tickets he found were for the end of May at The Music Box in Cleveland. We enjoyed similar groups, but they tended to lean toward more of a folk or bluegrass category. After listening to a few of their songs, we were hooked. Their harmonies blended perfectly in this Americana-folk-rockabilly kind of sound.

The concert date is here. My dad, my sister, my husband, a couple of family friends, and I piled into Dad's SUV that afternoon and drove north to enjoy the evening—dinner and a show.

As we laugh and banter back and forth in a vehicle full of self-proclaimed comedians, there is something unsaid. Not everyone knew about the change that had occurred. Or the irony in the timing of seeing a group called *The Secret Sisters.*

I enter the venue in a bit of a daze and in awe, as if I am entering some sacred space and need all my senses to be aware of the divine messages I may receive. *Why did we discover their music just last fall? Why were they in Cleveland only a couple weeks after I told my dad?*

I whisper to Dad, "There's only two of them up on stage, but you've got *seven!*" He smiles knowingly and his eyes go big as a response to me, and I know he has that surreal feeling too. It's all still sinking in. Seven secret sisters.

As if their band name wasn't fitting enough, hearing them live is like hearing a soundtrack of my grandma's life in those years. *Had they learned about Evelyn and Wilma's stories before Jen and I ever knew?* I silently muse. The sisters seemed to be telling us our grandmothers' stories in song form right here on the stage in front of me. Their newest album, *You Don't Own Me Anymore,* shows the sister songwriters' grandmother as a young woman on the cover. Songs about keeping secrets, bad habits and bad men, heartbreak and loneliness, pining for love or childhood again. I try to smooth out the goosebumps on my arms.

I imagine them and us decades ago in the same place with the same music. They'd take requests and Evelyn would ask them to do a cover of Eddy Arnold's version of "Make the World Go Away"—perhaps dedicated to both her and to her old friend, Wilma Eckstrom.

Wilma

Evelyn

119

CHAPTER 18

THE REVEAL

June, 2017

Dad and I decide that we need to meet with Uncle Frank and Uncle Jim about their results soon. The sooner the better. At the start of this, I assumed I'd be forwarding an email of their results and that'd be about it.

To prepare for the meeting, I spend time gathering my notes. I make a spreadsheet showing the centimorgans and ethnicity estimates comparing each brother. I make three copies of the notes I took, three copies of the records from the courthouse, online databases, and add those to three binders. I print out images for visual comparison and any other "evidence" uncovered in the past few weeks.

The day is here. I stand in my parents living room, alone, waiting for everyone to arrive. It was never this quiet when I was growing up. The silence makes time go slow and my thoughts echo from ear to ear. I feel all color drain from my face and my grip tightens around my bag, the three neatly assembled binders in front of me like a shield. I think of Grandma holding her large black purse on her lap, waiting for someone to give her a ride home. She always seemed ready to get home.

Off the living room is the former dining room, which now serves as a space for the piano. Family photos sit on top of it and plus more hung on the wall directly above. Two large windows let light spill into the room and onto an L-shaped window seat. I make my way over to it and sit down.

Through the window the flower garden soaks up the sun as house wrens, finches, and cardinals stop by the feeders full of seeds and thistles for a quick bite or to swoop into the bird bath for a cooling dip. The coneflowers and bee balm sway calmly as a small breeze tiptoes around them. I break my gaze from all the peaceful things just going about their business, wishing our lives were that carefree and simple.

The wood grains of the coat closet door draw me into my childhood imagination: two ghostly Perriot-like figures with large eyes and skinny bodies frozen in a dance-like pose which they had held since I was five. Shadows, clouds, tree bark, patterns in the ceiling at the dentist's office... there are places where hidden objects and hidden faces reveal themselves if you stare long enough. Clouds and shadows change and fade, but the occupants on the coat closet door of my childhood have remained. I've never been able to unsee them.

I stand up before my thoughts swallow me up and make my way into the kitchen for a glass of water. The sound of the garage door gears squeaking and pulling it upward immediately knots my stomach. My parents are home from work.

Mom opens the door from the garage. "Hi there! I think they're all on their way." She starts flipping on lights, getting the house ready for company. Ever a quick draw at hospitality, she throws a new tablecloth on the table, sets aside a few glasses and small dessert plates. I suppose it's just in case they want an appetizer before I serve them a hearty helping of the truth.

Dad arrives and places his work bag down next to the hutch where it's always gone. He smiles at me with eyebrows raised and asks if I'm ready for this. Yes. Ready for it to be over. The real question is, are they ready? Will they accept it? I have a front row seat to witness grown men hear for the first time how the things they knew about their mother, childhood, and relationships to each other have been altered forever.

As my mom and I stand in the open floor-plan dining room and kitchen talking about how we think they may take the news, I hear the first victim knock on the front door.

"I'll get it," I say. "I just wish my stomach would settle down."

She reassures me as I dart past her, "It'll be fine! It is what it is." My stomach doesn't care to obey my mother; it's still firmly in knots. Dad heads to their bedroom to freshen up after a long day at work.

It's not as humid and sticky as other June days, but I yank hard on the front door anyway. It opens with a whoosh. I smile too big and say "HI!" too loudly. Uncle Frank greets me with a hug as he steps into the living room, and I tell him he can head into the dining room and have a seat.

"You've got me worried," he says with a chuckle and a half-smile, making his way into the kitchen where I hear him say hello to Mom. I keep the front door open so I can see out the storm door window to the driveway.

A long minute passes and Uncle Jim's vehicle pulls in. At the door, I repeat my awkward greeting, shut the door behind him, and lead him to the dining room. They are now both cracking jokes with Mom, but I'm in another land trying not to visibly shake. Dad is back and I pass out the binders as everyone sits down.

"Now, no one look at them yet," I say as open binders around the table quickly shut.

I begin much like I had with Dad: charts and facts, but I start with Jim first. It will establish the Lawrentz connection when they see the certain matches he has (like Robin's), though the amount of DNA he shared with each of them won't raise any red flags yet. After a couple of minutes with Jim's test, I move on. Everyone wants to see pretty pie charts.

"Go ahead and look at the page with the chart; that's the ethnicity estimate."

"Oooh, I have 1% Iberian Peninsula!" one exclaims. I'm sure my uncles are still wondering why they had to meet in person to get this information. Then we move on to Dad's results.

I talk about his match with Jen and how we began messaging back and forth, stumbling on some unexpected information. I ask them to note that Jim doesn't share Jen as a match, and how Dad doesn't share a match with Robin or any of the other Lawrentz matches that Jim has on his list.

Now I have their full attention.

Silence.

I hold my breath and let the news sink in.

Suddenly laughter, almost giggling, fills the room. Sounds that one might hear at the junior high cafeteria table, for instance. And the jokes start flying.

Their childhoods were difficult and mostly unstable, and yet they seem to be amused that it was even more bizarre than they knew. With a hesitant half-smile, I sigh in relief and feel some confidence replace a little of my anxiety.

"Linda (Linda Eckstrom, I mean) remembers playing with *our* Linda. She remembers Grandma making them fortune cookies with little papers inside of them, passing down clothes, being kind to them and to their mom Wilma..." I show them the postcards addressed to the Eckstroms and the 1961 picture of Aunt Linda holding Carol's baby.

"You know..." says Uncle Jim, "I think I remember the Eckstroms! Them coming over to play cards or something—I remember being kinda bummed. All these girls came over to play with us... they had no boys in the family." He smirks. "And Leon—I remember him bringing over a briefcase full of siding samples. I'm sure it was for Mom's crafting supply!"

Jim continues to share as memories surface. He recalls his mom putting music on her record player and how she would dance around the house.

One day, he was coming down the stairs and saw her dancing with some guy, maybe a family friend, maybe a salesman. He ran to get Phil's handgun to scare the guy off.

Frank snickers and looks at Dad, "Of course this would happen to you!" They all laugh, Dad looking ready to blurt out our next surprise.

I jump in and say, "Okay, now hold on. Uncle Frank, why don't we look at your binder." With the attention now focused on the youngest brother, he scans the first few pages. I ask them to notice that he doesn't share DNA with Jen either, so he isn't a match with the Eckstroms. They sigh with uncertain relief. Then I ask them to note that he also doesn't share the Lawrentz matches that Jim has.

The realization hits my uncles and groans fill the room. Like a bad pun dawning on them. The ultimate Dad Joke.

"So," I continue gently and state what is now obvious to them (because someone just has to say it), "these facts lead me to believe that Phil is also not *your* dad, but neither is Leon. At this point, I'm not exactly sure who is. The promising news is that you do have a first cousin match—this E.K. person," I look down and reference the info that was also in my binder, "and that person is not a match with Dad or Uncle Jim. That's where I'll start—I mean, if you decide you *want* to know..."

That is something to consider. He may not want to know. After all, when they woke up this morning it was anticipated that they'd meet with me to explain some tidbits about their European heritage, maybe with a trace of indigenous blood to add validation to old stories.

Both of my uncles seem to be lighthearted and accepting of the news. Still, I want to give them space to process. The three brothers had been left in the dark, believing things foundational to their identities and relationships with each other that weren't even true. Had it been my duty to tell them the truth once I learned it? I had asked myself that question over and over again.

Uncle Frank, in his best Oliver Twist impression, looks over at me and jokingly pleads, "Please, Ali, find my daddy!"

They drop comments about it making sense because of some of their personality differences and looks. Now, anyone can tell they are related, but speculation on which features came from where had swirled around for years.

Dad has red hair (now almost all white and gray), and is the tallest of the siblings at 6' 2". Plus, a big personality to match. Aunt Linda was the shortest, a highschool French teacher with kind eyes and a kind smile. Uncle Jim has an average build, brown-auburn hair and a more slender nose like Linda's, conversational and involved in the community. Uncle Frank, who'd always claimed to have blocked out his younger years and jokes about being adopted, is the youngest of the family. He has the most introverted nature of the brothers, is shorter than Dad, with broad shoulders and jet-black hair that's now peppered gray. "This is crazy—so we all have different fathers!"

I jump in: "Well, you were all raised by the same Dad—Petermo!"

A chorus of agreement sounds around the table as we wrap up what I'm sure has been one of the most unexpected meetings of their lives.

Standing, Uncle Frank looks at me and refers to his comment, the joking plea to find his father. "Really, I don't care if you find out. It's okay." With such a close match for him in the AncestryDNA matches, the likelihood of finding out the truth is more of a reality than I think he realizes.

Uncle Jim and Dad start naming husbands of the couples they remember coming over to play card games like Euchre, Pinochle, and Poker, speculating the possibilities of who Frank's real father could be.

CHAPTER 19

FATHER'S DAY
June, 2017

With both uncles informed, it's a relief when I heard back from Frank's closest match's test manager so quickly. A man named Jerry had replied to me and explained that "E.K." is his wife, Ellen. He is the family history buff in their family and says he'd be willing to talk to me if I'd like and includes his phone number.

If she is truly Uncle Frank's full first cousin, that would mean his genetic father would have to be one of her uncles. On her mother's side? Her father's? A glance at her family tree may lead us right to him.

Clementine started taking piano lessons from a college student earlier this summer. We don't have a piano at home, so the student arranged for us to meet on the university campus and use a practice room in the Arts & Humanities building when classes aren't going on.

It's lesson day. The plunking sounds made by my bright-eyed five-year-old echo and bounce off the cinderblock walls just as they did every week we showed up for lessons on the third floor. Occasionally, a music major pops in or out of another practice room, gripping the handle of their instrument case. Plenty of rooms are still unused, and I have half an hour to scroll through Facebook, read a book, or stare into space. I'm quick to avoid phone conversations, but my curiosity is stronger than my aversion, so I decide to call Jerry.

Slipping into a nearby practice room, I shut the heavy wooden door with a skinny window donning its top half. The room has one long window that looks down on the beautifully landscaped campus. A plain-looking oak piano hugs the cinderblock wall in the tiny room. Pulling out its wooden bench, I sit down, like hundreds of times before at the piano of my childhood home.

While we all had degrees of natural ability (like Dad) to play and sing music by ear, he wanted his girls to learn how to read music. So my sisters and I took piano lessons and joined the children's community chorus in Ashland. We'd go on to join the orchestra, band, and choirs in middle and high school. Theater, music, art, and sports filled up most of our teenage years.

I place my AncestryDNA notes next to Jerry's phone number on the music stand as if it were sheet music, pull my phone out of my bag, and take a breath. Time to talk to another complete stranger about something personal.

He answers the phone after just a couple of rings. Our signal isn't the greatest, and I can tell he has me on speaker phone. I focus and strain to hear his words, trying to reply as clearly as I can.

Jerry shares that he's at the Wendy's drive-thru and is coming up to the ordering speaker. I smile. He must have deemed my call important enough to still answer right when it rang.

I can hear muffled conversation as he places the order for himself and his wife into the drive-thru speaker. Jerry (in his late sixties) has plenty of stories. His interest in how DNA can shape our understanding of genealogy is something we already have in common. He's endearing and pleasant to talk with. Any left-over trepidation I had from the beginning of my call fades away.

I fill Jerry in on how my dad and my uncles took Ancestry DNA tests which turned up unexpected results. I mention how the matches shared by all three brothers were *only* on their maternal side which gives merit to the conclusion that they each had a different father.

"But now I need to figure out who Frank's father is—I believe the answer may be within your wife's match list. Could one of your wife's uncles be Frank's father?" After adding in some dates and locations for good measure, I shut up.

Cautiously, Jerry gives me a little bit of his wife's family story: a few names, places, dates. I take quick notes—at least enough to do some digging later after my little Mozart is done with her lesson. I thank him and he assures me he will look into what he can about the matter. I can tell he really will follow up with me. We have the same inquisitive nature: interested and intrigued by the next mystery to solve.

Research hour at my house is when the kids are finally knocked out and stop coming out of their rooms to ask for a glass of water or say some sweet thing to us, knowing full well they can't get in much trouble when being so cute. Research "hour" is also a subjective term. An hour usually turns into three or four; eventually around 2 AM finding myself with contacts stuck to my eyeballs, my feet (as well as my rear-end) tingling with pins and needles, and thoroughly regretting my terrible choices. But I am a grown-up, darn it, and I can stay up as long as I want.

Tonight, I'm focused on plugging all the information I have on Ellen from my phone call with Jerry into the Ancestry search fields. Yearbook photos quickly appear in the results. "Well, they are definitely related," I mutter to myself. The dark hair, the eyes, a friendly laid-back and tight-lipped smile. I save those images, glance through the search results, and find a few obituaries. Pieces of the family tree form in my mind and I grab a pen to draw it out on the pad of paper next to me.

Now, I need dates and places of both birth and death for each of Ellen's uncles. Her mother's family has three potential males. Her father's side, just two. Looking at her dad's brothers' birthdates, they are *so* much older than Grandma. While possible, it doesn't seem likely either of them could fit the profile.

I look at her mother's brothers. The oldest, born in 1915, the middle son in 1925 and the youngest: in 1927. The family lived in Columbus, Ohio.

I'm interrupted by a new email notification. It's an invite to view Ellen's family tree. Jerry must be working on genealogy tonight, too. I click *"Accept."*

The family tree I quickly sketched out on my notepad matches what I'm seeing on Ellen's. I click on names I am quickly becoming familiar with. Attached to the names of Ellen's mother's side are pictures. One is a family group photograph showing her grandparents (outside of the service station they owned) standing with Ellen's mother, their other two daughters, and three sons.

The photo doesn't indicate who is who. I recognize Ellen's mother from other photos. I stare at the three sons. Brothers to Ellen's mother, and uncles to Ellen. The faces and bodies of people I don't know and am not related to. I pause at the young man to the very left of the image. Though it's a black and white photograph, I can tell this man's hair is either very dark brown or black, his fitted white t-shirt reveals broad shoulders, his arms crossed behind him. He's handsome, with a pronounced jawline, barely a smile and deep-set eyes.

I type out a message to Jerry to ask if the man with the dark hair is the youngest brother, Theodore.

"Yes, that would be Uncle Ted," Jerry replies.

I learn that Ted played baseball in high school, went into the Navy, was an owner of a business in Columbus, and had five children with his first wife. They were married for 48 years before they divorced.

Though I am struck by Ted's looks and that he is closest in age to my grandma, I keep notes on all three of the Rector sons. While Jerry and Ellen share more information with me, I also find my own from census records and city directories online. The middle son moved to California in the early 1950s, but the oldest and youngest stayed in the Columbus area. In the directory listings, all three men were listed as salesmen.

Father's Day is here. It's only been a few days since the "reveal party" at my parents' house. Though my burden of being the sole keeper of the secret is gone, I can't help wondering how they feel about this particular Father's Day. I have the perfect card idea for my dad. I grab my laptop and open an image of Leon from the 1960's. Jen had shared it with me a few weeks ago. Looks like it was taken at a portrait studio.

Wearing a tie and jacket with a decorative pocket square, he had a serious and confident yet almost bored look on his face. His demeanor seemed very professional and straight-laced, with smart looking glasses framing his face and a receding hairline.

Is that ring a wedding ring? It doesn't look like any wedding ring I've ever seen. His arm draped over the other in a standard portrait, the large ring decorated his left hand and rested over the middle of his right forearm. He had kind of hairy hands with long fingers just like my dad.

Next, to the Googles! Ah, a random photo of Darth Vader. That will do. In Photoshop, I crudely cut out the helmet and head part of Darth, layer it to rest on top of Leon's suit jacket covered shoulders. I find the perfect Star Wars-like font and type out:

MIKE, I AM YOUR FATHER.

I hit the print button, it spits itself out and I fold it in half, writing a half-sentimental note on the inside, and finish by signing my name. I can already hear his animated exhale-laugh and high pitched "HA!" he does when he is surprised by something he thinks is hysterical. I smile, feeling grateful that I know my father and he knows me.

❦

My phone rings. It's Jerry. I tell him my hunch: one of Ellen's maternal uncles is my uncle's father. He isn't sure that any of them would have had an affair but couldn't be sure. He says he'll investigate it a bit more and talk with Ellen.

The very next day around the same time as the evening before, my phone rings.

Jerry again. I answer.

"This is the most confusing thing we've encountered!" He continues. He says after giving it some thought, they agreed that Ellen's Uncle Ted might very well be Frank's father—if they have to pick one out of all the uncles. It makes enough sense to them. I think back to the picture of the family Jerry shared with me and remember the broad shouldered, black-haired youngest son Ted.

I think we found Frank's daddy.

CHAPTER 20

LOST AND FOUND

Present Day — June 2017

[OUR UPDATED FAMILY TREE]

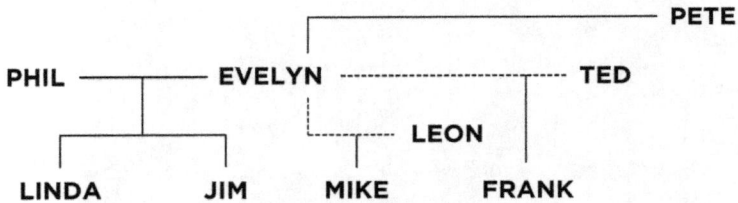

```
                                                      ┌──────── PETE
                              ┌───────────────────────┤
    PHIL ──────── EVELYN ─────┼────────────── TED
                              └──── LEON            │
           ┌────────┐         ┌───┐
        LINDA      JIM      MIKE      FRANK
```

I drive south on 71 and hold back tears. Glancing in the rearview mirror confirms my superficial fear: a puffy, blotchy face stares back at me. A just-hold-it-together fail.

But why should I feel like I have to hold it together? I'm about to experience a moment (though perhaps inconsequential for some) significant enough to warrant big feelings. Meeting my new cousin Jen for the first time is a moment I want to keep in my heart memory forever.

Communicating online for months, we have this chance to meet face to face—an Eckstrom and Lawrentz together in person after almost sixty years apart—it felt monumental, a culmination of all the years of secret keeping and truth silencing. A simple DNA test and a couple of postcards began the unraveling of a story that may have never seen the light of day. This powerful reality is what continues to moves me to tears. But, if she thinks I'm a weirdo, it could kill any chances of my dad getting to meet his sisters. Dear God, please don't let me be a weirdo just for this afternoon—or let her be a weirdo too so she won't know the difference.

The sign for Panera gets closer and I make the exit. Pulling into the parking lot, I grab my phone and notice Jen left me a message. She and her daughter were there early and grabbed a spot in the back by the fountain soda machine. Okay, here I go. I reach for my purse, take a deep breath, and head inside—stomach flipping the whole way. Long lost cousins, yes, but somehow it feels like being separated at birth and reuniting.

I scan the space near the back like she mentioned and spot them at a booth by the windows. She sees me and we wave at each other, smiling, and I walk toward the table, hoping I don't trip over my own two feet. She's wearing black and white, and I have my black shirt with tiny white polkadots on. We hadn't even called each other to match.

"It's so great to meet you in person!" We hug.

"Hi, Mia!" I say to my little cousin who is my own son's age. Jen and I have seen pictures of each other, of course, but getting to experience the characteristics of our shared DNA in person made everything so real. With familiar eyes, face shapes, and freckles, she was also born a redhead. As we chat, I notice we have a similar way of talking. She must notice similarities too; occasionally she pauses to say how I remind her of this relative or that relative. People she's been around her whole life and grown up knowing. Family get-togethers, weddings, funerals, graduations. We weren't at theirs and they weren't at ours.

My throat is tight again as I analyze the other possible outcomes of this secret. My dad, my sisters, and I come from a part of their family's past they may have wanted to forget. Yet here we are, a generation or two removed from the circumstances that make us related, our existence now known and inserting ourselves into a family that was already going about its own business. We came out of seemingly nowhere. We are trespassers.

I feel ashamed that it hadn't occurred to me that this whole ordeal could have been a total disaster that came filled with rejection and a resurgence of bad blood. My nature is to err on the pessimistic side, though I like to call it being realistic. Even so, I know I can be naïve, and once I'm on board with something, little can stop my energy and positivity for it. But if the rest are anything like Jen, we won't need to worry. She's warm and welcoming, and has no guard up with me at all. It feels like we've known each other for a very, very long time. In another life where we grew up together.

"I have something for you!"

She pulls out a stack of papers. It's a collected family history. Copies compiled for me that include names, dates, old Swedish records, pictures of ancestors, and more. She wants to bring me up to speed on my new lineage. What a gift for us!

"This is amazing. Thank you, Jen!" I flip through a few pages and a dramatic black and white photocopy of a dashing looking man in his forties or fifties brings my flipping to a halt. His intense eyes stare back at me.

"That's our Second Great Grandfather, Gustav Ekström from Sweden." Jen points out.

I had deleted my Lawrentz branch weeks earlier, but I now have something to replace it. Something that is real and true.

I also have something for her. Less warm fuzzy feelings with this material, but still interesting to us both: copies of Leon's court records from my trip to the Mansfield Courthouse.

We sit in the Panera booth like we are college roommates cramming for a test. I ask her questions, she answers. I take notes. She fills me in on family stories and whose children are whose, locations, occupations—I struggle to keep it all straight but listen intently, mentally downloading new familial information. I can then share what I am learning with my dad, sisters, nephew, niece, and my kids. We are now their people, and they are now ours.

Oh, and Leon? He stood about 5' 11".

It's been a few weeks since Jen and I met in person. She said when Leon died in 1999, he was cremated, and his ashes were spread over his parents' graves. They were buried in Lexington, but he had no marker there. And no obituary, for that matter. Lexington isn't too far from Ashland, so I load up the kids and drive twenty minutes to the memorial park to see if I can find the burial spot of my great-grandparents, Carl and Helen Eckstrom.

I arrive, but I don't feel like asking for help or plot numbers. I want to see if I can find them myself. Trekking around cemeteries isn't a new thing to my kids. They've never asked too many questions when we'd take them—I don't think it phased them to know that caskets of skeletons were beneath their little feet. When they were even younger, I'd have to contend with them climbing on bigger headstones and a certain son of mine asking if he could pee on one because he couldn't hold it anymore.

Suddenly I spot it.

ECKSTROM in raised serif lettering on a bronze memorial plaque, flush to the ground. Decorative roses border a small banner that said *Together Forever* etched onto the plaque. Carl died in 1982 and Helen in 1996.

I reach for my phone and tap the camera app open. "Miles, Clemmie, come over here...yeah, stand right there behind it...okay, say cheese! This is where your great-great grandma and grandpa are buried!"

They cooperate for all of two seconds: enough time for me to capture a few pictures. Their prancing around continues, exploring the grounds nearby. I linger at the Eckstroms' resting place and wonder about them.

"I'm your great-granddaughter, Allison. You have two more great-grand-daughters and our dad is your grandson." It feels dumb to introduce myself and talk out loud to the memory of a couple of people, but I do it anyway.

And while I have no idea how to begin reclaiming the past, coming to Oak Grove Memorial Park this afternoon seems like a good start.

CHAPTER 21

ACCENTUATE THE NEGATIVES

July, 2017

A few weeks ago Uncle Frank mentioned he owned a nice light box out at the shop I could use if I needed to. Eager to scan more negatives, I decide to take him up on the offer today and make my way to the office.

I pop my head into his office and say, "Don't worry, no more spit tests!" He laughs as he gets out of his chair and walks to a shelf where the light box is located. He removes it carefully from the case and hands it to me along with the power cord. I thank him and set up my space in the conference room.

Lights out. Light box on. I pull the cigar box full of negatives from my bag and begin taking them out of their sleeves slowly. I place fifteen or so on at a time and attempt to not get distracted by figuring out who or what is on them. The goal is purely take pictures of each filmstrip with my phone and inspect them later. It's hard to wait.

Even inverted as they are, I can easily make out pets and people in the negatives: that's my dad, that one is Grandma, their old dog Jake, Aunt Linda...I am now an expert at picking them out just by body shape or hairdo. Their faces, clothing, teeth (when they showed them), and their

ALLISON LAWRENTZ BARNHART

body language. I'm making great progress. It's only been a half hour or so and I'm just about through them all. I think there are around six hundred-some images. Editing is going to take some time.

❧

It's been a few days and I've been itching to get a closer look at these negatives. Saturday night in mid-July and nowhere to go. Perfect evening to nerd out on my negatives project. Inverting from dark to light. Over and over with each photo from the negative strips on that light table.

Immediately I recognize some images because they exist as printed pictures that I've seen many times. Some aren't as familiar, but I know the people and the places so I save them out. I edit them one by one.

Open.

Crop.

Invert.

Save As.

Close.

My muscle memory kicks into my fingers.

Command+O, Command+I, Command+Shift+S, Command+W.

Command+O, Command+I, Comman—

My insides flip. I'm no longer a key command machine. My eyes scan the image, frantically trying to place it.

I quickly open Facebook Messenger to contact Jen. It is nearly midnight. How do I get to sleep now? Especially if she doesn't answer and I have to go to bed without her input.

At the light box a few days ago, I remembered seeing this exact negative, this exact figure in its inverted state and assumed it was my grandma. It was Evelyn. I was sure it was her.

But I was wrong.

This woman has wavy, light-colored hair. She sits on a quilt, legs straight out but crossed at the ankles, supporting a baby with one hand, and with the other, giving the baby a bottle. Mostly in shadow, the image shows the bright light at her back so that the baby in the ruffled dress she's feeding is covered in shade. She looks as if she was in mid-sentence or not quite ready for the picture to be taken.

The sunlight paints her shoulder closest to the camera—her skin blinding white in grayscale; the dark shadows of tall trees reaching long across the grassy space. It must be a hot summer day: the woman wears a sleeveless paisley print sundress and open-toe strappy wedges and, in the distance (just beyond a creek bank), sits a bench full of baseball players at a ball diamond. The catcher crouches behind home plate. *Looks like Brookside Park in Ashland.*

I have never seen a printed photo of this image in my grandma's albums or loose in a box before. I type to Jen what I have been doing with the collection of negatives and ask about this photo.

"I found this photo (negative) of a lady with a baby. Something makes me think it could be your grandma. What do you think?"

I upload the file and the image sends. There are more images to go, and I can't invert them fast enough.

To my relief Jen is online. She replies right away. "Wow! I need to show my mom to confirm but I can see the similarity. I will see my mom and Aunt Debbie on Sunday. I really think it is her. Do you have a date?" I don't have a date, but I may have the next best thing.

I feel a wave of satisfaction—in the same strip of negatives that holds this possible image of Wilma Eckstrom, there is an image of my grandma with a baby I *do* recognize. My dad. It must have been taken the same day.

This photo of Grandma and Dad is one that my family has seen many times. It's a printed photo in an album. She is standing near the road at what seems to also be Brookside Park, wearing a summer dress, holding my dad in her arms at her side. He was a large baby, and in this picture, I would say he's under a year old. Since it was obviously taken on a warm month of the year, Dad could have been between five and nine months old. Both photos, Wilma with baby and Evelyn with baby, had to have been taken in the summer months of 1960! But, who took the picture of Grandma and Dad? Wilma? Aunt Linda?

It's even more obvious the images are from the same day because of the additional negatives in this same grouping. One shows Dad: a five- to nine-month-old baby Mike in a walker next to another baby also in a walker beside a park side picnic table. My dad wore the same clothes as in the photo with his mom holding him. The other baby wore the same ruffled dress as the baby on the quilt with the woman we think is Wilma.

And then *another* picture of the two babies, and then *another,* and *another.* Eventually the outfits change, and it looks like a different place, a different day. But the children? The same. Dad as a baby and the same baby girl. Goosebumps run like a current up my arm. This *has* to be the youngest Eckstrom daughter who was born a day after Dad. It's Karen. I upload them to Jen as fast as I can.

Tears fill my eyes and my heart pounds, moved at the thought of seeing them both together. Proof that brother and sister had met before any memories of each other could be engraved in their developing minds.

Jen got the images. She types "...the hair on my arms stood straight up...chills..."

Of course in my mind, the moment Grandma realized she was pregnant she would have cut off contact with Leon and simultaneously the friendship with Wilma. In real life, things just aren't that simple.

In the other images I just sent to Jen, Dad and Karen look a whole year older. The contact between the families seemed to continue through the summer of 1961 when the two were around 18 months old. Walking, swinging, hugging, and even kissing toddler kisses to each other. How do these images I'm seeing even exist? So sweet and loving and completely mind-blowing.

Two more images inverted show three kids standing on a sidewalk, a white sided house is the backdrop. I've seen that siding before. Looks like the Lawrentz' Walnut Street house. Little Michael Lawrentz, looking absolutely delighted next to two little friends: the one I now recognize as being Karen, the other—could possibly be the second youngest Eckstrom sister? Jen agrees, it's Debbie. Sisters disguised as family friends, the secret sisters of a secret brother.

They'd been taken from each other and were never told about each other's exisistence. And there was no plan to tell them. Too young to remember ever meeting. Fifty-seven years have now passed. How could Grandma have snapped pictures of them—maybe even directed them to hug and kiss each other and never mention it again?

Then again, how *could* she mention it? When would the timing have been just right?

A *tenth* negative catches my eye. Like the others, I send it off to Jen. Another park setting, another picnic table. I only recognize my Uncle Jim and Phil in the photo. The rest aren't familiar, but it's obvious to me that I'm looking at yet another impossible image of a past that everyone was supposed to forget about. The unfamiliar figures: two young girls in headscarves, a woman also in a headscarf preparing food, and a man in a fedora and sunglasses, wearing a white short-sleeved button-down shirt and a wristwatch. He sits across from Phil.

I had seen picnic shots of my Grandma's before. I'd recognize family and extended family (mostly the Bowers-England clan) or would notice some of the same friends or neighbors we heard about our whole lives. But these people? I have *never* seen or heard of them before. The young girl closest to the camera has glasses and reminds me of my sister at that age. I have a feeling I am seeing a moment that Evelyn chose to capture showing the Eckstrom and Lawrentz families together.

My feeling was quickly affirmed.

Like a family history ninja, Jen replied, "Picnic table photo is my grandma, Leon, and either Linda or Sylvia with the glasses on. My Grandma had bad ears and always wore headscarves when it was windy and made the girls wear them, too."

All of these photos are haunting images of a past I never knew, and a past my dad wouldn't have remembered. I can't stop staring at the picnic table scene and put myself in Evelyn's shoes. Behind the camera, again, capturing the moment. A beautiful day in a park to have a picnic. A couple of young girls—daughters of your friend—sit at the picnic table eating their sandwiches, and across from them sits your son drinking some juice; next to him: your friend, Wilma. Next to her, on the far end, your teetotaling, two-timing husband Phil, and sitting directly across from him is your friend's husband, your husband's friend, your siding salesman, and the father of your third child.

Did she owe it to us to tell us? Would I have told my children and grandchildren one day if I was her? She could have a hundred reasons to never tell, and I already have a hundred reasons I don't blame her. Maybe her way of telling us was silently through her photos and collections.

What if it went like this: the moment Grandma realized she was pregnant with my dad, she moved right into denial and compartmentalized it all. Her new truth would be that it never happened. The baby she carried was Phil's. *I'll name him Phillip Michael Lawrentz.* That's what it takes to survive. It could be that she was in love with Leon (or at least infatuated) and continued the affair for a while. Whether he loved her or used her is anyone's guess. The reality is we will never know.

Exhaustion finally finds me. It's now past midnight. Just one more message. Jen replies to an eleventh and final inverted negative exposure of film for the night.

This last image shows two little girls (both about three years old) at a picnic table with a octagonal metal sign that says, "NO PARKING HERE".

"To add to the emotion, it just *turned my birthday* at midnight! Can't help but think this is a gift from my grandma. Will show this to my fam. Also, we are getting together next Friday night to talk through Ancestry stuff. They are excited to see all the photos you've sent of your dad and family..."

She adds, "I just noticed the number on the picnic table is 36—this is my 36th birthday!"

The words "ENJOY DO NOT DESTROY" and the number "36" are stenciled on the supports under the table.

Jen thinks the one closest to the camera and smiling is Debbie. The other girl, with an innocent yet blank look on her little face, just stares at the camera with big eyes. Neither one of us recognize her at all.

CHAPTER 22

LITTLE BOXES

July, 2017

She playfully sets a bottle of wine on Jen's kitchen counter and laughs. Karen points at the Seven Sisters brand label on the wine so they all can see. Underneath the label, scrawled in black sharpie reads: *And one brother (that we know of!)*

The day Jen had her mom and the rest of the Columbus area Eckstrom sisters over for an ancestry reveal meeting of their own, I waited nervously to hear their feelings about the unexpected situation.

Jen had already filled them in with the basics individually, over the phone, over text, but she wanted to get them all in a room and go through the whole story: the evidence, the science, and the photos. They could react together viewing pictures of my dad—their brother—and their three new nieces.

The sisters confirmed that the girls from the negatives were, in fact, images of themselves. Debbie even remembered seeing a copy of the couple of photos with her and Karen on the sidewalk; the little boy, who had been so happy to be standing next to them had been cut out when the images became pasted in a scrapbook by their mother.

History repeating itself? A mirror image of a father with his three daughters a generation apart. *Image on left:* Allison, Elizabeth, Mike, Samantha—1996 | *Image on right:* Sylvia, Leon, Linda, Carol. Abt.1953

Leon had all those girls while the boy who got away was following in his father's footsteps. At least in becoming a salesman and having all daughters. When Jen showed me a few pictures of the first three Eckstrom sisters together as young girls with their dad, it was as if we were playing out a rerun of history—a reflection of the past. The first born daughter to the far left and far right, next the youngest sandwiched in between the eldest and their father, then the middle daughter tucked under his arm.

Meanwhile, there are still more things to go through. I finished processing all the 600-some film negatives, but there are boxes of postcards and scrapbooks and pictures that call my name yet again. It's my evening ritual.

A postcard featuring a mid-century kitchen catches my eye. Not a vacation card... strange. All the rest are.

The print on the back top left corner reads:

Custom Wood Kitchens—Built-in Appliances
Our Specialty—Complete planning, fabrication and installation service.
Ferrell-Gardner Wood Products
Phone 9-1575
New London, Ohio

No stamp, no address, or post mark but there's a stamped name and address on the far left and sideways in smudged blue ink:

LEON ECKSTROM
GENERAL CONTRACTOR
1594 WOOSTER ROAD MANSFIELD O
PHONE PY 3-7261 COLLECT ANYTIME.

You had me at "fabrication," Leon.

✼

Dad and I thought we should fill Mae in on everything. We are catching everyone else up, so it seems like the next best step. If it still didn't jog her memory, she may at least be interested to know. She was, after all, Grandma's oldest friend and the only person still living that knew what life was like for both of them all those years: before marriage, during marriage, and divorce.

So, I call her. I offer to pick her up and drive us over to meet Dad at a spot we all know well: the Lyn-Way Restaurant. A local family restaurant that has been an Ashland fixture since 1951, it will be the right kind of atmosphere for such a meeting.

As I help Mae out of the minivan, Dad greets us in the parking lot and holds the door for us to walk inside. "It's so good to see you, Mike! How are Mindy and the girls?" Mae had known Dad his whole life, and I knew Dad saw her as another mother figure. The greeter seats us at a table not too far from the exit; Mae at my right and Dad across from her. It's more crowded than I thought it would be. We make small talk and simultaneously skim the menu, Dad mostly updating her on the company and what my sisters are up to.

I wait for our server to take our orders, so as not to be interrupted. And possibly to avoid any chance of memory derailment or a crumbling comfort level in which Mae might shy away from sharing anything new. With a triple scribble on her notepad, the server is off to the kitchen, and I waste no time. "Mae, we want to fill you in on some things we've discovered lately about Grandma—and about Dad."

"Oh?"

Dad meets my eyes across the table for cues. An odd feeling of role reversal hits me as he follows my lead. I pull out my binder and a handful of pictures. I hand her the image of a two-year-old Debbie Eckstrom seated with the little girl that Jen and I didn't recognize that night.

I had showed it to Dad prior to our lunch with Mae. "That looks like Mae's daughter, Sherri." he said. "But Mae doesn't remember the Eckstroms..." I reminded him.

I study Mae as she studies the photo. *Do not destroy,* the picnic table warned. There were plenty of pictures with Mae and Evelyn's kids together, so finding others in which my dad recognized Sherri was easy. We compared the photo in question to those images we knew Mae's daughter was in.

Mae squints at the photo, confused. "Well, that is her, isn't it? Now, I can't say who the other girl is..."

"That's Debbie Eckstrom. When I stopped by for a visit, do you remember me asking you about the last name of *Eckstrom*? Debbie was one of their youngest daughters, and we just recently found all these new photos in Grandma's stash. There were some of these Eckstrom girls, and in this one Sherri happens to be with them."

Was any of this jogging her memory? Or maybe memory wasn't the problem. How hard do I push an elderly lady to divulge information from a pact she could have sworn to keep with her best friend?

"Mae, you know when I told you we knew of the name *Eckstrom* because of an AncestryDNA test Dad took? At the time I didn't quite know the extreme closeness of the connection. Well...it turns out that Phil isn't Dad's real father."

"No!" she says with a mystified expression, as if she was witnessing a plot twist of her favorite show.

"Dad's biological father is a man named Leon Eckstrom. Debbie, in the picture here, is one of his seven daughters. Leon had sold Grandma and Phil siding for their house on Walnut Street—Grandma and his wife Wilma became friends. Of course I really don't know about the order of things."

I want to move right into the postcards and what Linda Eckstrom had remembered, but I let Mae process for a moment, watching her confused face turn to surprise, amusement, and then quick acceptance.

She looks at Dad. "So Phil's not your dad, Mike!?"

"Seems not!" He says, laughing.

"Well! My goodness...I knew about the *first* one, but I didn't know about *this* one!"

Dad and I look at each other, wide-eyed and half in shock. I thought he might fall out of his chair. *The first one? The first one? The first one what? What is she talking about?*

I try to stay calm and give her time to explain.

"Evelyn and I were neighbors when we lived in that duplex on Miller Street... our husbands were over in Germany..." She pauses her story and chuckles. We don't need help filling in the blanks, but she continues to tell us anyway, and we listen. Intently.

"Evelyn had always been a bit of a wild one!" This might meet more of my definition of "wild" than when Grandma had shared about Phil's mom Sylvia and the spaghetti house.

Now, Lyn-Way is known for its pies, but at the moment I don't want to order a pie. I need something stronger. Like vodka. And I will share it with Dad. I'm thoroughly convinced Mae isn't keeping any decades-old secrets for my grandmother.

Once we relocate our eyes back into our sockets and chins from the table, Dad and I continue gingerly with our interview. "So you don't remember her mentioning the Eckstroms or seeing them around?"

She thinks. "Hmm, no I can't say I remember him or them—but that is my daughter, so she was definitely there with them, wasn't she!?" Mae glances at the picture again, looks at Dad, and starts processing through the circumstances as memory allows.

"Well, you know...your mom babysat both my kids for me occasionally since I worked...I bet she watched them and took them with her to the park with this other family. Probably walked or got a ride. Evelyn never did take to driving. She told me when she was sixteen someone took her out driving and she ran into a tree! I would have been lost without driving…"

Mae returns back to her surprise at the news. "I just can't believe she never told me about this one. I knew about that first one and how Phil was… back then there just wasn't much you could do…"

Another half hour of reminiscing about the 1960s sneaks by and it's time to go. As I drive Mae home, I thank her for having lunch with us and being willing to share her memories.

"Now, you keep me updated if you find anything else. What a story!"

"Oh, I will! Thank you for everything, Mae!"

After getting her safely inside, I hop back in my minivan and ponder over the last hour of conversation. *Wild*. Wild? It wasn't exactly the adjective my dad or I would have ever used to describe my Grandma Boreman before this lunch. Shy, kind, gentle, helpful, submissive, funny, selfless, slightly stubborn, slightly judgmental, and maybe wistful or melancholy… but not wild. A person could be all of those things, right?

"Ohhh, I'm too old to spoon," I recall Grandma telling me at some family gathering years back. I had only asked her if she wanted a spoon for her dessert. The slight smile and twinkle in her eye gave away her delight at having slightly shocked me with her witty joke. Whether it was at family gatherings when being offered utensils or spending time with her one on one, her unassuming dry humor accompanied an endless supply of puns and anecdotes. A regular goofball. The accepted source of this wit within the family was her father. It was the kind of comedic nature that's passed down. Goofy. Dry. But never wild.

In typical old lady fashion, she'd pass out cough drops from her purse whether you needed one or not, eye those young'un's tattoos with much concern, and encourage you to have a third helping. Plus, passing you a fiver for "being a good kiddo." She was a grandma who gave me an out-of-context Bible verse written on a scrap piece of paper when I got my nose pierced because she didn't think it was right; a grandma who was always ready to teach you a thrifty craft or show you the newest clipping from the funnies. "Didja see this one yet?" she'd ask as she pulled out the newest "Family Circle" joke from the stack of newspapers next to her chair.

When I try to imagine her beyond the grandma-persona, I do recognize the more vivacious version of her in those younger photos; the ones taken before all the hardships of adult life piled up like a collection of stones in her pockets, when she was still vibrant and uninhibited. Untamed. Maybe wild.

Then in the images that lead up to the divorce (while still posing in a new dress she made or in shorts and a crop top), her expression becomes consistently less carefree and with infrequent smiles. She gets her picture taken all the same.

I gather the photos spanning her twenties and thirties that find someone else behind the camera and inspect them as a group. Out of all the fitted dresses and swimsuits, here's Evelyn in a smart white shirt with ruffled sleeves and wide-leg black pants. She's outside, sitting on a chair, resting her left ankle on her right knee, her right arm propped up by her left with fingers placed gently on her cheek, a flirty smirk on her face as she looks at the camera. It's hard to tell exactly where she is or who she is with, but she seems confident and satisfied. Tough and unshakeable.

Those descriptions are immediately contradicted as I remember other photos I pulled out of a box recently. A group picture of her and her co-workers at Cresco Manufacturing shows all the ladies gathered behind a group of sewing machines in the warehouse. Only where she is, her face was missing from her body. It had been poked out by a pen, or a needle. I remembered the yellowed tiny piece of scrap paper with a silly face drawn in pencil and pasted over her yearbook photo from her junior year of high school.

Then, as she continued to age, so many photos were either a tiny thread of a smile or just a bit blurry, where a hand jolts quickly up in front of her face, hoping she made it in time before the person pressed the button down.

❧

As Mom and I find time in our schedules, we meet in the truck bay of their business warehouse to plod through storage unit items. This particular

Tuesday, we decide to take on another pallet of containers. The sweet but putrid smell of mildew hangs in the air at all times. Yellowed newspapers and magazines waiting to be cut out and pasted in scrapbooks rest their tired spines in boxes that climb far above my head. It's a test of dexterity and focus to sort them out.

All sizes of boxes line the pallets, and a shoebox catches my eye. I think of a story Grandma once shared with me. The number 24 was a special number because the day in the month of her birth was 24, her parents were married in 1924, and exactly one year before her birth, on the 24th of January, a baby girl "was born asleep" to her parents. The cord had been wrapped around her neck. A couple years prior, when they still lived down south, the first heartbreak of their family took place. My great-grandmother had given birth to stillborn twins. They buried them in a shoebox. "There was no money to do anything else, and back then," Grandma reminded me, "that's just what they had to do."

In my "keep" pile, amid all the brittle and stale, I notice a *Mansfield News Journal* paper that is dated Thursday, January 7, 1960. Anything from the 1950s and 60s are *KEEP*—everything else goes to the dumpster at the edge of the bay opening. I know this 1960 date is around the time of Leon's forgery court proceeding from my *Newspapers.com* research. I pause from the job at hand, lift it from the pile and scan its pages.

On the middle of page two, just to the right and down from the weather forecast, reads a small police record: *"Leon G. Eckstrom, 38, of 1159 Wooster Road, forgery; two counts."* I can't know for sure why she kept that particular edition but then again, why else would she have kept it? Perhaps the *"Calls For New Efforts To Curb Inflation: Ike Sees 1960 As Most Prosperous in History"* story? Sure. Or, if I'm giving her the benefit of the doubt, the specials advertised by O'Neils Department Store? Doubtful. Could be other articles—or notices from others she knew in that day's edition?

My fingers now dirty with ink, I pull a white piece of paper torn into a small square from a pile. Scrawling pen spells out *"Courtney Lee 12:42 A.M. 7.3 oz"* and *"10:05—8.7 oz girl Allison Rae."* Mae's granddaughter Courtney and I were born on the same day in March 1984. Grandma loved that we were birthday twins, she had told me. Later in life I would become friends with another granddaughter of Mae's—Sherri's daughter Sonja.

Beyond the menagerie of artifacts stored in that dock, I salvage a Polaroid camera, a 1956 Brownie Hawkeye camera, assorted Avon jewelry and glass perfume bottles, some costume jewelry, plus 1940s Valentines and Christmas cards given to her from schoolmates and relatives. Surprisingly, all in amazing shape.

Alternatively, the items being thrown out consist of: Dried out Artex and Tri-Chem paint tubes and supplies, what looks like smut books entitled *The Magnificent Obsession* and *Three and a Half Husbands,* empty cigarette cartons, a plastic hand for a doll still in its blister pack, and a large cardboard box filled with dozens of empty white paper boxes, lids intact.

I lift a book from the "Throw Away" pile. *Alimony,* printed in 1945 by Faith Baldwin. I threw it in the pile a minute ago, in a machine-like trance but also because of the condition of its pages—as if a mouse had gnawed away at the trash novel's chapters. Maybe I'll have another look.

Flipping it open, I realize it couldn't have been the work of a mouse. I make out the shape of a small revolver. No X-ACTO knife seemed to be harmed in the making of this hollowed out piece of fiction. It was either done in a hurry with blunt scissors or someone had no intention of exhibiting high-level craftsmanship and dug at that thing with a rusty old spoon. On the back inside of the hardcover is a pencil tracing of the handgun.

I can't decide which would win in a battle of the bizarre: random revolver-shaped hollowed out space within a vintage romance novel or the dead animal in a shoebox that turning out to be tangled clumps of hair. I had jumped and shrieked, almost giving my mom a coronary.

I find some treasures, too. A loose page torn out of a magazine featuring an in-color beauty shot of Maureen O'Hara, a small catalog from Union Hardware in Ashland about home decorating, a thick book of wallpaper samples with some of the coolest and ugliest prints you'll ever see in your whole life. *Keep, keep, keep, and keep.*

Next, I discover autograph books that weren't sold off. Presumably unsold because they were names of non-famous folk, schoolmates, and relatives.

> *"July 3, 1960: Dear Mom U R A very sweet mother, and I'm sure there's no other as sweet and lovely as thee, and I hope you'll always be. Your loving daughter always, Linda"*
>
> *"Dear Evelyn, I wish you health, I wish you wealth, I wish you gold in store. I wish you life after death—what could I wish you better. Be a good girl, obey your parents and walk in the way the Lord would have you go. Obey the Lord for this is right. Grandmother Lizzie England"*

In some of these notebooks, she also had sayings she hand-copied out of books or magazines:

> *"If at first you don't succeed, cry, cry again."*

> *"A conscience doesn't keep you from doing something, it just keeps you from enjoying it."*

> *"It's a great life if you weaken in time to have a little fun."*

> *"Men! If you smile at him he thinks you're flirting, if you don't, he thinks you're an iceberg. If you let him kiss you, he wishes you were more reserved; if you don't he'll seek consolation elsewhere. If you flatter him he thinks you're simple. If you don't he thinks you don't understand him. If you talk of love and romance he thinks you're asking him to marry you. If you're a good girl he wonders why you're not human. If you return his caresses he doesn't want you to, if you let him make love to you he thinks you're cheap. If you don't he'll go with a girl who will. If you go out with other fellows, he thinks you're fickle, if you don't he thinks no one will have you. Men....God bless them they don't know what they want!!!"*

The Family Weekly magazine sent out by the *Mansfield News Journal* from May 31, 1964, is tucked away in yet another scrapbook. The front-page highlight article titles reads *"When a Husband Is Unfaithful by Dr.*

Paul Popenoel."

I pick up a small green diary out of the piles of boxes still left. I have a glimmer of hope that it's a diary that somehow escaped the journal-inferno of the late 1960s. No such luck. I open its cover and it's a journal of Grandma's she kept before marriage and before kids. A five-year diary dated 1941 through 1946 where she simply jotted down a couple of sentences of what happened each day. Inside the cover is typed "Five Year Diary - Memory is elusive - Capture it!" The teenage voice of my grandma resounds off the page, a voice I have never heard physically, but can imagine clearly.

Pressed flowers and four-leaf clovers, dried-up stickers, and ticket stubs occasionally fall to my lap as I gently turn the frail pages. But the postcard scribbler had struck again in this diary. The ink makes the same harsh loops, like coils of barbed wire along words and half-sentences she must have deemed incorrect or embarrassing. Few are legible, and as in many moments of discovery this year I can only go so far down their plentiful roads before something, even something as small as ink, obstructs my view.

❧

I may not be able to do this ever again. One of three things will prevent it. Schedule, lack of courage, physical ability. I inhale deeply through my nose and allow myself to start sinking under the surface of the chlorinated water.

It's the end of summer and I'm at the appointment I had made earlier in the year. I hadn't chickened out. Insecurity and guardedness tried to shut it all down, but I tuned out the voices, still eager for the unique experience.

A local photographer was offering short underwater sessions as a way for him to experiment and practice with the underwater lenses he bought. I felt like I should sign up for a session, well aware that just because I was an okay swimmer and a fan of *The Little Mermaid,* it did not equate to my being photogenically successful underwater.

Nevertheless, because I like to be prepared, I picked out a flowing dress, pinned glam underwater shots to a private board on Pinterest, had regrets about not having let my hair grow out longer first, and finally lamented the thirty pounds I had put on since having children.

Just before my descent to the bottom, I joked with him about being more buoyant than I had been ten years ago. "I will definitely need those hand weights you brought to do any sinking!"

The other people scheduled to be photographed were 17-year-old high school students looking for unique senior photos. I'm just an out of shape mom out of her jeans, out of her van, out of her element. Maybe it's the first time I recognize I'm not "young" anymore. But I'm not old, either. I kind of still feel sixteen.

I try to shut off my insecurity but can't help but feel utterly silly for having imagined myself as Anne Shirley imagining herself as the "Lady of Shallot" and how wonderfully melancholy and romantic it would be. Minus the boat with the hole in it.

Nevertheless, I didn't need a leaky rowboat to sink into the water. I disappear beneath the blue, weighed down into the deepest part of the pool. Strands of hair ebb and flow above my head with no choice but to follow suit and descend with the rest of me.

As I settle to the lowest depth I can go, I feel like I'm in this ethereal moment—suspended in time—only my copper locks and the aqua dress with a cream-colored lacey overlay remain unfixed. It's odd—the pressure down here feels loud and overbearing in all of its silence.

What's really taking place is that I'm trying to have a relaxed look on my face, while attempting to control hair and fabric from its natural watery dance. My lungs start to burn. It's possible two seconds haven't even passed. I drop the weights to the bottom for the shot and in no time my buoyant-self floats effortlessly to the surface.

There's something about the water. My ancestors were sailors, watermen. My painting entitled *Silenced* featured an underwater scene. I had been baptized in water. I made-believe I was a mermaid in every pool, pond, and lake I swam in as a girl. It can calm, cleanse, encourage creativity, and it can terrify. Water is part of our ongoing story.

The photos were fine. None turned out to express what I saw and felt in my mind during the shoot. After he sends the touched up digital photos to me, I look at them for a minute but can't stare too long. I fight embarrassment. I order a few prints to have proof of my moment as a mermodel. All of them simply contained my authentic submerged poses, in all their awkward glory. As if it matters, I vow to myself to never quit my day job to pursue a modeling career, especially an aquatic one. But it *doesn't* really matter. I did it for the experience. I did it for myself and for my grandma. For Evelyn.

I wonder what my grandkids will say when they find those photos in a little box someday.

CHAPTER 23

ALTERATIONS AND MENDING

September, 2017

My uncle sighs anxiously as we turn into the parking lot of The Rusty Horseshoe. Jerry and I had arranged a lunch meeting at the Mount Gilead restaurant since he and Ellen were in Columbus visiting friends. Seemed to be a good half-way point for both parties.

"Doin' okay?" I ask Uncle Frank as the four of us hop out of the SUV. "It's not so much the goings on..." He thinks for a moment. "It's that she just never told us..."

We make our way to the entrance of the restaurant and Frank holds the door for his fiancé Ranee, granddaughter Lexi, and me. We quickly scan the dining room. No sight of a couple fitting the description of his cousin and cousin-in-law.

"You can take a seat wherever you'd like," a server says as she hurries past us, balancing a tray of dishes collected from a recently vacated table.

Needing a clear view of the parking lot, we claim a spot by the window with seating for six.

I begin to share a couple of reassuring thoughts about my interactions with Jerry when I see a vehicle pull up. Illinois plates.

"I think that's them!" I exclaim, interrupting myself.

A middle-aged couple gets out. Suddenly I feel nervousness I hadn't before. The weight of responsibility finds me even though they aren't my genetic family. Could I guarantee my uncle would have the same positive experience in meeting a new family member like I had with Jen?

As they enter, I see the same curious yet nervous faces on Ellen and Jerry. They spot us, and we wave as they head toward the table. We push out our chairs to stand and greet them with hugs and handshakes.

God bless Jerry (a man after my own heart), he came prepared. Pulling out a laptop from his bag, he places it on the table like an appetizer and we get right down to business.

With orders placed and delivered to the kitchen, we start leaning closer to Jerry's computer screen as he clicks through the pictures he carefully collected in a folder full of Ellen's family history.

Next, Ellen opens a manila folder to show her newfound first cousin loose photos and then an album of the family. Her grandparents, her mother, aunts, and uncles. A belated introduction to Frank's family.

I brought pictures as well. Sometimes without comparing images directly it's hard to see resemblances. With the Rector family pictures still out on the table, I place photos of Frank from childhood to young adulthood next to the images of Ellen's Uncle Ted, Frank's presumed father.

They all gasp.

The same look of mischief captured in their eyes, the shy smile, a gap in their front teeth, and on each: a full head of dark hair.

Frank, 1984   Ted, Abt. 1946

Jerry digs in his bag and places a couple of business cards on the table. They are Ted's. The first: *"T.G. Rector—Electro-Hygiene Co., 453 Miller Ave. Columbus, Ohio"*. Then one with a cute little sewing machine graphic at the top right: *"Dressmaker Sewing Center—Sewing Machine Distributors, Sales and Service—"Ted" G. Rector, Sales Representative, 19 East Rich Street, Columbus, Ohio"*.

Uncle Frank and I laugh out loud and gather ourselves to explain to them why we may have the answer to Evelyn and Ted's paths crossing. Evelyn the seamstress would need a sewing machine, wouldn't she? But I could only guess about how they met back in early 1962? Over the phone, at her front door on East Walnut, or maybe they knew of each other through Cresco years prior and reconnected somehow? All I know is I'll never look at siding or sewing machines the same way again.

Time passes quickly at our table and lunch finishes up. We snap a couple of pictures of the cousins together. "We'll be in touch," Ellen says, hugging Frank goodbye. "And we'll encourage Ted's kids—your siblings—to get DNA tested so they can see for themselves. Then we can be 100% sure the connection is with Uncle Ted and not one of my other uncles. But from the look of those pictures..." We laugh knowing that while having the DNA brings us full certainty, it would be shocking if we have it wrong. Ellen and Jerry both hug me too, like I'm also a part of their family. We all go our separate ways, but a sense of victory stays with us.

Frank had found his daddy.

November, 2017

And Mike had found his sister. Found her standing in his living room now staring at him, meeting as adults for the first time. I stay seated on my parent's couch and watch as Susie's husband Ron, along with Jen and Mia make their way through the Lawrentz front door lining up behind her. As we welcome them in, Mom closes the door, the wind blows fiercely on the other side.

Just over a month after Uncle Frank met his cousin Ellen, Dad is now getting a chance to meet one of his seven sisters. Susie, a short red-haired lady with a hopeful and contagious smile, stared up into the eyes of her 6' 2" little brother. The house gives a fleeting rattle from a clap of thunder.

"How are ya!?" he says invitingly.

She replies with a breathy and nervous excitement. "Well, hello!"

"Good to meet you!" Dad continues the polite ping-pong of greetings as he gauges whether to go in for a hug or if a handshake could be more her style.

A gust of wind claps at the siding. I glance out the window to see a sickening yellow sky.

Their demeanor toward each other is gentle and cautious. But quickly, Susie seizes the moment and hugs him. With a laugh and a lament, she sighs, "Better late than never, I guess! Where have you been all these years?"

"Right here!" Dad says, grinning.

The instances I've seen Dad smile like that was when he got to hold each of his grand babies for the first time. Just like those deeply kairotic moments, this one also held the tension of both fear and excitement, colliding like the warm air rising through the thick cold of the weather condition currently materializing outside.

I begin to cry. Tears of joy, relief, grief, all of it. There had been so many critical moments in this year full of discovery, but this one—seeing them meet after more than fifty years—the last piece of damaged and timeworn plaster breaking away from the original art underneath. Ready for its restoration from years of darkness, the full light could shine in, and it shone in on us.

We weren't supposed to meet any of them. I broke the rules of the secret. The forces of nature outside don't seem too pleased with me either.

As our new family makes their way further into the house, my sisters, our husbands, our kids, and my mom also greet the four of them. Smiles, hugs, and quick introductions are given as we all settle in.

"We can all go into the dining room and enjoy some cake!" says Mom, as she directs traffic and thanks Susie for the spice cake she brought. The kids quickly hit it off and were downstairs playing in a flash.

Immediately conversation turns to resemblances, Karen and Dad's birthdays, and "what if the younger sisters had met dad and dated!? They could have been in the crowd at some of his band gigs!" The table erupts into laughter thinking of all the what ifs.

After some time passes, I decide it's a good moment to do some show and tell. There were artifacts I constantly stumbled upon in the books and boxes of Grandma's things. In one such box, a few loose photos I had never seen before revealed themselves, and I could already tell they were from the 1950s-early 60s: monochrome with decoratively cut out edges.

I put one of the photos in my binder so I'd remember to bring it with me for the big meeting. Across the table, I hand it to Susie and Jen.

The photograph caught my Aunt Linda staring at the camera either annoyed, sad, or just not ready for the click of the shutter as she sat on the porch floor of the Walnut Street house beside another little girl. They seemed to be in the middle of playing a board game. This other girl reminded me of both of my sisters at around age 9 or 10. I quickly realized this must be Linda Eckstrom. Not the first image of the families I found, but the first one of the two Linda's playing together—and *that* gave full credence to the living Linda's memories she shared with Jen; the memories that put our investigation into high gear. Nothing written on the back like many other photos Grandma had, but the date it was developed shows JUN 1959. I could see the porch was now enclosed with siding (thanks to Leon and the Mansfield Siding Company). The two girls were in the middle of playing the board game *Sorry!*

Susie confirms enthusiastically, "Oh yeah! That's my sister Linda!"

I light-heartedly narrate: "Just sitting on the porch on Walnut Street... playing *Sorry!*"

We laugh as if the past was offering to make amends.

"They don't look too happy!" says Jen, with an amused, yet sympathetic tone in her observation.

Susie replies, "Nobody was happy back in those days!"

Desperate not to lose the show-and-tell momentum, I grab an article I recently scrounged up on *Newspapers.com*. I had already sent a copy to Jen. I hand Susie the printout and she interrupts herself and reads. After a couple beats of silence her voice rings out, "Oh my gosh!" She would have been nearly seven at the time of this article, and it featured her older sister's wedding announcement.

I knew Carol had gotten married young. I had the honeymoon postcards she wrote to her parents that were then given to the avid postcard collector, Evelyn, the family friend. I had found the picture of Aunt Linda (Lawrentz) holding Carol's baby son at the Ashland County Fair.

So when I had done a *Newspapers.com* search for their name, one of the first results to be listed was about their wedding in 1960 at the Main Street Evangelical United Brethren Church in Mansfield. As I read down through the column, I tripped over the same sentence that caused Susie to start.

*"...At the single ring candlelight ceremony, the Reverend C. C. Vandersale Mandrisal united in marriage the daughter of Mr. and Mrs. Leon G. Eckstrom ... guests were **ushered to their places by Mr. Phil Lawrentz** of Ashland..."*

For Pete's sake.

<hr/>

December, 2017

The snow is still coming down, but we made it to Columbus. After the successful reuniting of one brother and one sister, we had four more sisters in the area to re-introduce to their long-lost brother.

Jen's home is a revolving door of relatives as we gather for the Christmas party. And they can't miss Dad walking in. The tall Viking-sized spitting image of their old man almost scares them. Nevertheless, in seconds a frenzy of chatter, laughter, and squeals ring out and Helen, Debbie, Linda, and Susie are hugging him, and my throat gets tight. The way they are delighted to meet him makes me feel like I will melt into a Frosty the Snowman or Olaf puddle right there on Jen's living room floor. They find my mom, sister, and me and pull us close, too.

The front door opens again, and it's Karen. She makes a beeline for him and hugs him for a long time, saying, "I've got a list of names for you!" Playfully ordering him to take his stature and status of big brother seriously.

"We finally got somebody to stick up for us!" says Debbie. Helen chimes in, "I told Michael there was always a piece missing from the puzzle; now everything's come full circle." Susie recounts her first meeting with us a month earlier to the group as Karen brings him a red shirt to put on over his sweater, one that matches the shirt she's wearing.

"Because we are birthday twins," she explains. Her shirt reads "KEEP CALM I'm the Little Sister" and Dad's says "KEEP CALM I'm the Big Brother".

Like the Lost Boys examining the grown-up Peter Pan/Peter Banning in the movie *Hook,* the sisters study him unapologetically and interrupt themselves with observations and charmingly unfiltered comments as we all stand in the open hall space between the kitchen and living room.

"You have his eyes."

"Green with blue and gold flecks."

"And nose...and his whole face!"

"The same red hair..."

"I think it's all meant to be."

"You are very much wanted, Michael."

"We're all just so lucky to be well adjusted enough to receive this kind of information!"

Linda speaks up from her chair in the living room, "I feel sorry for him having to meet *all* these people!"

We listen as Debbie and Helen tell us the *Cliff Notes* version of our Swedish heritage. Karl Ekström left Sweden in 1914 to avoid Swedish military service and start a new life in America. Three other Ekström brothers immigrated as well, all coming through Ellis Island. Some of the Swedish family would come to the States and visit them but Karl never got back home to Horn—he would never see his mother again. The only communication was writing letters.

While in the Army, Debbie told her grandfather she would visit Sweden for him since he was too old to attempt such a trip by that time. And she did that very thing. Five times over.

Concentrating on every word of her impassioned retelling of her travels, Debbie is careful to pronounce any Swedish word properly, with umlauts and rings in all the right places.

I am overheating and sweaty yet completely engrossed in each of their stories and questions. I barely pause to graze the delicious looking holiday foods and treats that were set out all over Jen's kitchen counter. As much as I want to fuel back up on sugar cookies, meatballs, and cheese, I don't want to waste an opportunity to learn something new about our history. I keep putting my drink down who knows where.

Awkward silences do not exist this evening; if there is ever a moment that feels like you can experience making up for decades of lost time, it's this one. Nurture is absolutely a strong force, but here we are witnessing how forcefully nature brands and binds us. Time stands still as the surround sound of strangers who look similar, talk similar, and laugh at the same things fill the house.

I was naïve to assume the reunion would be all nice and lovey dovey. I can't believe I hadn't considered they could reject us and would have every right to. Be skeptical of us. Be bitter and hold a grudge for their mom, for themselves. Take one look at my dad and refuse to get past that he looks just like the father who hurt them, who left them.

Of course, they had wondered about these things at first. Would he be just like Leon? How did he turn out? I'm struck by the realization that they had been able to take a leap of faith, face the ghost of their father with courage, and choose to see beyond it to the person they see before them now. Their newfound brother, Michael.

Something shifts in my dad. I know he misses his sister Linda Louise. There is no replacing her. But there is this sense that a part of our collective family's healing process has developed into a new phase of repair.

Dad sits beside Linda Eckstrom, and she tells him a few things. "I'd stay overnight at your house. We'd go to church together, and I hung out with her, you know, when the families would get together. 'Cause both our names were Linda, and we were close in age—everybody's name back then was Linda," she quips.

"Did you remember my brother, Jim?" Dad asks.

"Oh yes, I remember a little boy running around with us girls. When you were born, I remember coming over and your mom, Evelyn, had a sign at the bottom of the staircase that said *Shhh—Baby Sleeping!*"

Dad laughs, "That's right! When Mindy and I started having our girls, each older sister would be taught to say 'Shhh, baby sleeping!' Like I heard from my mom and that sign!"

Linda continues, "Oh, I remember your mother was good to us. She would take us to drive-in movies, and she would make hot dogs that she'd wrap in foil for us to take along. Evelyn was good to my mom, too; she gave her clothes. They came over almost every week and we'd make two chickens. We did all this stuff outside, had picnics...she was a very nice lady. She was a good housewife and good mother."

"I wouldn't have traded her," says Dad proudly.

"When did she pass away?"

"She died in 2009, on Jim's birthday."

"Did she have cancer?"

"Well, she did, but that was under control. She got Parkinson's and that slowed her down a lot. We thought she'd like the social life in the nursing home, but she didn't participate. We couldn't let her stay alone in her house though, because even though home health aides would come and her friend Mae would come to visit, she wasn't drinking water or taking care of herself."

"Oh, I'm sorry to hear that."

I take the pause as an opportunity to shift the conversation and address the unspoken apprehension that may still surround the circumstances for being family in the first place. Linda is straightforward.

"I admit, at first, I felt a little bad when I heard about you all, about Michael. I felt hurt for my mother, like meeting you all might not be loyal to her. They were friends, Evelyn and her. But my father," she looks at Dad, *"our* father could talk *anybody* into *anything.*" She nods to herself as she remembers.

"He was voted best salesman in Mansfield for ten years in a row. He could sell you anything and he could sell himself." She explains how he battled with addiction and mental illness. Bipolar, she thinks. The word "sociopath" is thrown out there. His younger brother Carl was thought to have suffered from Schizophrenia, and we were told he just kind of "disappeared." The addictions Leon fought seemed to surround alcohol, gambling, and women. Or, in Linda's order: "Women, wine, and the races."

She tells us about the night she went to the front window to watch her mother learn from the police that Leon was arrested and headed to jail. "That's when everything was going on." I realize Linda is referring to the forgery. When Leon was being held in jail (before his trial), he received letters sent by a woman that signed them "Your Lonely Tiger." The letters were given to Wilma from the police, and Linda is convinced they were from Evelyn.

I smile, not wanting to dismiss her earnest notion, but skeptical of my grandma being the author of letters signed with such a suggestive pet name. Then again, I hadn't see my grandma as Mae's "wild" best friend, either.

"She's not the only one," Linda adds, to reassure us that Evelyn wasn't unique in being lured in by Leon's charm. Other women were used and taken advantage of. I feel a misplaced twinge of heartache; I don't want to see her as a victim again, but I don't want her to have chosen a path of infidelity—even if she *was* married to Phil.

My nagging question tonight: Did she become friends with Wilma before or after the "relationship" with Leon was happening? Would that make a difference? Would it help us categorize who is more hero, villain, or victim in our drama? I don't like to think she had a part in betraying her friendship with Wilma and in turn Leon betraying Wilma time and again. But ultimately only those three would be able to tell us what happened.

Let's say the fact of *when* Evelyn met and became friends with Wilma didn't matter. Of course, I'd like to imagine there was *some* love involved when it came to her and Leon, but understanding how he operated and how most women unwittingly crossed his path helps Linda (and perhaps the other sisters) have more compassion than resentment for their mother's friend Evelyn. They had forgiveness and empathy ready for her when confronted with the reality of our existence.

Both Wilma and Evelyn lived with impossible strife during their young adulthood and child-rearing years. Both longed for support and significance by having a family of their own. Both wanted the love, happiness, and stability that such a family was supposed to bring—especially in an idealized post-war America.

Linda continues. Leon always had a woman on the side. "My mom must have known about Evelyn eventually—that must have been hard," she adds. "They had always wanted a boy, and if she *knew,* maybe she thought 'now he gets to have one with Evelyn.' They were going to name a boy Richard Eric, if they ever had one."

She tells me how their mother would ask her to report back to her when Linda went along with him to one of his girlfriends' places. "When I think about it now...that was such a bad position to put a child in.

"But he had *many* of them," she seems to have an effortless recall as I listen to her rattle off memories, "and many other children...In Ontario High School there was this girl my age (in my class) and I thought, 'She looks like me and my sisters!' When I asked my mom, she said, 'Oh yup, that's one of his.' He had got this lady pregnant, and she gave the baby up for adoption to some rich people..."

A year and a half into the five-year probation sentence, Leon had received permission to move their family down to Columbus. He had been offered a job at North American Rockwell as an engineer. That was 1961. By 1968, their daughter Sylvia would finally convince Wilma to leave Leon for good and gave her the money for a divorce.

Wilma remarried a man who would treat her well and take her on trips. But from time to time, she would ask the girls if they knew where Leon was or if they had heard from him. She had been with him since high school and would be forever connected to him regardless of their estrangement.

I ask Linda about her memories of Leon's parents, her grandparents.

"Well, his mother (Grandma Eckstrom) was Helen Matilda Magnus, and she used to cook for rich people in mansions in Illinois. She and Leon were very smart." Linda continues to explain how their grandmother Helen went to business school and became a purchasing agent for Higbees and Macy's in Cleveland. She remembers Grandpa Eckstrom, Carl, loved drinking whiskey and eating sardines in his living room chair.

"Those Swedes had delicious baked goods, but they liked a lot of not so good things like sardines and smoked fish," she muses.

"Linda!" Susie summons her older sister to answer a question about a Christmas gift one of her grandkids just opened. "Linda, where'd you find that stuff? Anderson's is gone..."

"At a craft show," she replies.

"You went to a craft show without me?" Susie fusses kiddingly with her.

"I got lost. I went by myself and got lost!" They josh back and forth like sisters do as we shift seats and mingle with another bit of family to try to catch up on a lifetime of lost time.

I brought my binder, and along with it, many photos, mostly of Dad as a young kid, so his sisters could see what their big little brother looked like growing up. A scrapbook that Wilma had put together for them years before sits next to mine on a table. This must be the one Debbie referred to in recognizing a picture I had from Grandma's collection. I leaf through it and ask my aunts if I can snap pictures of the pages with my phone.

Busy flipping through the binder I brought, Susie snickers. "Karen, when you and Michael are old you can reenact that picture with the walkers!" She holds up the one of them as infants looking at the camera, wide-eyed in their baby walkers at the park.

I spot a very old picture of a family from the early 1900s in Horn, Sweden. It's a picture of Grandpa Ekstrom's family, they tell me.

"This picture cracks me up," Karen points to the children. "I know it was the old days of pictures, but we always think it looks like something from *The Shining*, it's creepy! Look at those little girls!"

Then a familiar picture appears, cut out in a circle: two little girls on a sidewalk, a white sided house behind them. I shake my head in disbelief. There is a little boy missing from this photo. The photo Debbie recalled.

Wilma had cut it out for placement in her daughters' scrapbook and their half-brother stood just far enough to the right of them on that walkway for easy removal. The double of this photo had been given to her by her friend Evelyn, who kept the negative that I would find decades later.

The buzz of lively half-stories of past and present, good-natured interruptions, and spirited laughing finds every corner of Jen's home combined with a soundtrack of classic Christmas tunes playing in the background.

Debbie picks up a framed 5x7 photo to show me. It's a picture of an old man, legs crossed and holding an unopened present. His posture, the shape of his hands, the length of his fingers, the specific expression of his eyes—even down to things like his dress shirt and khakis—they're familiar. An epiphany washes over me and takes with it all color from my face. Debbie confirms the hunch.

"That's Leon."

It's as if I'm looking at a future photo of my own dad.

CHAPTER 24

FOR KEEPS

July, 2018

"The Mind...is a wonderful machine. It need but be just refreshed and incidents can again be revived in their former clarity. A Line...each day, whether it be of the weather or of more important substances will, in time to come, bring back those vague memories, worth remembering, to almost actual reality." *(from Grandma's high school diary front cover)*

Ali, you won't believe what we found in Grandma's stuff.

I reread the text on my phone as we make our way from a trip in the North Carolina mountains back to Ohio. Having "closed the case" on the Eckstroms and now the Rectors, I have been more focused on building relationships with our new family, which amount to around fifty members (significant others included). But if there's more to be found, there's more to be found.

I call up my parents and ask if I can stop by. I drive the four miles north on 42 to my childhood home, turned the knob to the navy-blue front door, and shoved it open with the back of my shoulder. Another humid summer day.

"Hey! Alright, you have me all anxious—what'd you find?"

Out from the very last box in the storage unit load came a handful of black and white photos in amazing condition. They include prints of some images I thought I only had negatives of. In addition to those, there are images I'd never laid eyes on at all.

March 1959—more from the Florida trip—with Grandma playfully sitting in the basin of a pedestal bird bath, smiling in her two-piece swimsuit for the camera while two women looked on laughing at her stunt. One of the women is Phil's sister Bonnie.

Next, a group of photos from a June 1959 playdate at the Eckstroms, who had put up a small, above-ground pool. Jim, waist-deep holding a beach ball, and Susie is nearby, her face scrunched up and eyes closed tightly, floating on top of the water. Helen stands in the grass, watching. A little boy with his back to the camera is waist-deep in the water like his friend Jimmy. It's Chip, Mae's boy.

The next picture shows Uncle Jim again but standing to the right side of two women holding their babies. The women are clearly Mae and Wilma. Mae holding Sherri and Wilma holding Debbie, both infants. In their future, we'd see the same two little girls at the park picnic table. *Number 36. Do not destroy.*

More pictures from June 1959 reveal Evelyn and Mae laying out on a blanket with baby Sherri in the backyard of the Walnut Street house, complete with swimsuits and sunglasses.

Then, as if the rest weren't enough, images I only had negatives of before (the two snapshots of Dad, Karen, and Debbie on the sidewalk at the Walnut Street house) are in this last pile. On the back, Grandma had written two long dashes with question marks beside them and then "Mike Lawrentz." She had forgotten who the little girls were when she labeled these in her later years, as she spent her time sorting through her keepsakes. If she had remembered, I don't think she would have labeled it at all.

And finally, I pick up a group of photos that seem to be from the same day the jaw-dropping negative of the two families together at a picnic table was taken. My parents were right. I can't believe what I'm seeing.

An actual print of that very negative is in the mix along with a handful of photos capturing Leon, Wilma, Dad, Jim, Linda Lawrentz, Karen, and Helen or a combination of them together. As to when and where, my best guess is late spring/early summer of 1961 at the Columbus Zoo.

One shows the kids inside a monkey-bar-like "cage" designed to invite children to pretend they are zoo animals. Just outside the cage, peering behind the bars at the camera stands Leon in his fedora and shades. Another image shows a large wooden cut-out of a lion, jaws all the way open. Helen, Jim, and Dad are standing inside the mouth of this ferocious King of the Jungle—Grandma taking the opportunity for yet another entertaining shot.

The last couple of 2-½"x3" prints show Dad and Karen on a face-to-face glider swing set. Grandma had captured Dad staring at Leon, who seemed to be in mid-sentence and pointing or pushing the swing with his right hand. Gathered up and tucked under his left arm, he held on to a large blanket.

Did Leon know that the little boy, Michael, who stared up at him from the swing was his son? Did Wilma suspect (yet)? What about Evelyn, who just kept taking pictures? She had no time for questions or wondering anymore. Survival came first. Taking pictures was an inconsequential act. She had become a woman who wanted to keep doing normal things at all costs. The only way she could carry on would be to go all sub-rosa and not acknowledge secrets or the truth at all. Take your kids to the zoo with family friends, have a picnic, take pictures, and smile.

"This too shall pass," she used to say to me. And it had passed. Passed undetected through the decades. The pictures are more than I could hope for, even more than a year into the discovery. I can't wait to show Jen.

🐝

We met even more Eckstrom relatives. Over months that seem to melt into one wild family coming-of-age story, there were a handful of gatherings. A cookout, a restaurant, a bonfire, a shopping trip to IKEA. I met Carol's son and daughter, Susie's sons, Karen's sons, Linda's daughter, and Sylvia's daughter. *My* cousins. Not to mention many of their children and spouses. I learned so much—past and present.

During one of those visits, a story emerged of Leon having another family in Chicago.

Wilma filed for divorce in 1948, but Leon's mother Helen was determined to keep the family together. The narrative was that Grandma Eckstrom went to Chicago and "dragged him back to Mansfield." Wilma would go on to have the other four girls with Leon.

I learned that Susie's son Josh and his wife Kelly were crucial to the DNA puzzle early on. It had been Kelly's idea to buy Josh and Susie a DNA kit that Christmas. Each interaction gave us moments to connect with the past and present, a way to flex our new family muscles.

An intriguing tale Susie and Linda told me surfaced. They told me they heard that the "old man" had once "robbed a bank down in Florida." I hadn't yet spoken of the postcards Grandma wrote from Florida and Georgia; I merely asked her if Leon ever worked or looked for work in states other than Ohio. What did the quotations around the words "a job" in Grandma's message to Don and Gerri from that 1959 trip to Florida really mean?

Was it Leon *Eckstrom* who had been with them on the trip? Was it just an offhanded, teasing comment about a legitimate business deal or inquiring about employment? How will I ever know the truth for certain?

On the Rector side of things, the opportunity to meet up with two of Uncle Frank's half-sisters came about and I of course jumped at the chance. DNA tests through 23andMe put to rest any left-over uncertainty we had about the dark-haired sewing machine salesman. Ted was officially confirmed to be Frank's father.

"We heard from Linda and she indicated they are flexible and would like to get together. We told her that we wanted to meet with you if you would like to get together again. We are certainly looking forward to a visit."

Ellen and Jerry emailed and helped arrange another meeting, this time with a few new faces: another sister named Linda, her husband, and a sister named Jill. They were all friendly, warm, and gracious.

More pictures and stories were shared around another restaurant's table. I was greeted with friendly teasing.

"So you're the one!"

I laughed, but inside I hoped I wasn't giving myself an unwelcome reputation. If I was, it was probably too late anyway.

⚘

November, 2018

As I turn the slightly fragile page, a loose newspaper clipping wedged in the gutter of Grandma's scrapbook flutters and grabs my attention. It's the third, maybe fourth album in the stack I've looked through tonight.

I feel a bit frozen—literally. Not because of the clipping, but because I can't bring these musty things inside my house. We would all end up with terrible sinus infections so my garage will have to act as my investigation area for now.

I adjust my particle mask. Since I only have the dim garage overhead lights on, I grab my phone flashlight and hover it over the yellowed clipping. Dated Saturday, May 21, 1960, it's an image of a one-story duplex for public auction: 202 Miller Street. The very home Phil and Evelyn had moved to around 1955, and the very duplex they shared with Mae and Art. Looks like they converted it to a single-family house (whenever this was printed.)

Just under the photograph reads the caption "Love Nest." I let out a mask-muffled laugh and mumble, "Well that couldn't be any more perfect!" I continue flipping the edge-tattered pages looking for perpetual answers to secrets, smiling and commenting to myself under my mask. Hopefully, my incredibly attractive face accessory will keep me from becoming the army of mold spores' next victim.

Featured in a column on the following page, a young Carol Eckstrom places fresh linens on a patient's bed during her days as a "Volunteen"—a Junior Red Cross nurse's aide. It's a detailed article so it fills the whole 12"x14" page.

"'We really enjoy doing it,' remarked Carol Eckstrom, one of the Volunteens. 'I've been amazed at how much I've learned in the short time we've been

working here like this.'" The article even describes what their uniform looks like: *"Wearing the blue and white striped pinafore and white coronet chosen as the uniform of the Volunteens..."*

I don't even know what time it is. I know I can't stay out here forever, I'm freezing, my feet are tired of me standing, and my neck is ready to stop angling down to the old repurposed kitchen counter. An ugly fake marble—emerald green and plastic, I think. Two-thirds of my face is protected but my eyes burn and itch a little. I am not about to try to rub them with my mildewy rubber gloves. I should really wrap this up. I hate to even entertain the thought that I wish I didn't have even more to go through. Time is always an issue. It is also overwhelming.

"Okay," I sigh. "A couple more pages in this one and I'm done for the night."

There, along with a couple others glued in columns about engagements or weddings, lies an article about Carol's engagement and bridal shower in 1960. "Carol Eckstrom Feted At Prenuptial Shower" and "Will Speak Vows June 5 In Church". No photos in the printed articles, but I don't need them. I have plenty of those, and plenty of pictures in my imagination.

If I had never found any tangible evidence about the Eckstrom family before, I might be in disbelief with a find like these three clippings, but I am swimming in evidence—enough for me to chew on for years.

❧

End of Summer, 2019

I set aside my tea and open the photo album. Linda Eckstrom sees the picture of her little half-brother Mike, a chubby infant, propped up on the couch, a hard-part combover of red hair, and wearing a button-down shirt and a tie. She wryly comments, "Looks like he's about ready to sell some siding."

I giggle.

I invited her to have lunch with me so I could hear more about her memories of growing up and spend time getting to know her as one of the seven aunts I had been without. *"Ask me anything, I'll tell you anything you want to know about,"* she had insisted.

I drove to her Columbus apartment, picked her up, and we decided on Chinese cuisine. We arrived at Windchimes, one of her favorite restaurants, and asked to be seated in the back room where it was quiet.

"Oh, and that one," she points at a studio portrait of a seven-year-old Michael with his three Lawrentz siblings from 1967, "that one looks like Leon with the ring on his finger. Leon always wore this Mason ring... but he *even* got kicked out of the Masons eventually."

"Gosh," I say, as we finish with the album and pick at the rest of our meals, saving our fortune cookies for later on. "He burned quite a few bridges."

Linda sighs. "That Bob Mabee, who he went to school with—he was his lawyer—he said if Leon would have used his smarts for good, he would go really far. Like I said, it was the wine, women, and races that got him. When he got to Columbus, there were two horse racetracks, Scioto Downs and Beulah Park—so he was in heaven. He'd get so mad when he lost at the track!

"Part of the time Uncle Bill (who was my mother's brother) was his probation officer, so he could get away with more stuff. He once stole a car from a dealership he worked at; he stole other cars, but he also would sell people siding and then steal it back from them to resell it.

"My mother, she called them his 'flunkies'; dumb men that looked up to Leon—they would do whatever he said. So when he told them to pull siding back off people's houses or steal stuff for him, they would! He even stole siding off his own father's house! Can you believe that?"

I shake my head. Linda's stories remind me to ask about Leon's interactions with his parents. "In the records for the forgery case, his parents went to court with him and basically signed something that said they would lose their house if Leon didn't pay back what was stolen. So I wondered if they ever repaired their relationship...since in Grandpa Eckstrom's obituary in 1980 they don't even mention Leon. "Just one son, Carl, one daughter, Helen." There must have still been a rift for the family not to put his name in there at all."

"Well, our father—I told you he was an alcoholic, and he had untreated bipolar pretty bad, and probably OCD. He drank to self-medicate. Kept a bottle under the front seat of the car—straight whiskey in a flask. If I was in the car with him and he'd be going so fast, I'd just pray that God would keep me safe. His drinking got so bad, one time at a holiday get-together, Leon got to drinking and he beat his own father up outside. His own father!"

"Do you know if he had a good upbringing? Do you think he just had mental illness and addiction, or did something happen to him when he was young?" I ask. I hope she is still okay being immersed in these memories again. The curiosity I feel in learning everything I can about the terrain and trajectory of my grandfather's life plus the lives of my aunts is too powerful to stop my ongoing investigation because of any lingering timidity I may feel.

"I don't know. I had heard Leon was even violent as a kid; he hit his brother, Uncle Carl, in the head. They said Carl was a schizophrenic, and he would follow Leon around and Leon would take advantage of him... he didn't seem to have a conscience... but I also heard Grandma Eckstrom would lock them in a closet when they misbehaved.

"When his grandmother, Selma, died in Davenport, he went up there and went through the house for her money. She hid it everywhere, in the walls... and he tore that place apart just to take whatever money he could find."

Linda's list of her father's misgivings and flaws continues.

"After I was born, he left for Chicago and was basically there for five years. I think he changed his name to Lee and married somebody else...he had lots of aliases. That's when our mother was trying to divorce him, but Grandma Eckstrom brought him back to Ohio and soon after that Susie was born. She looked just like Leon; she was a beautiful red-haired baby. He'd put together swing sets for us but have us girls help him. He ended up hitting Sue in the head with one of the poles from it.

"He would get so upset if we helped him the wrong way. 'Hold this hammer!' And then we'd hold it for an hour til he wanted it."

I think about Grandma, Dad, Linda, Jim, and Frank and how, around the same timeframe and in the next town over, they were experiencing parallel abuses.

"Leon did put a pool up for us on Wooster Road. He liked the water. He used to jump in there and try to drown us," Linda continues, almost matter of fact. "Our mother wouldn't go in the water with him. She had told us that early on in their marriage he had tried to drown her. He tried to do away with her so many times...he beat her so badly..."

But as early as she can remember, she had lived with her aunt and uncle on their farm.

"I thought Aunt Eva was my mom for a while. I even thought my cousin was my brother. Susie lived there for a little bit, too. Once we were older, we went back home, but we were all scared of Leon. We would run to the playground and hide while he was home. I was always ironing his shirts, mowing the yard, and bringing him 'a cold one.'

"If he had us in his car, he would drive us by the orphanage and tell us how we'd probably all end up there. I prayed to God that it would happen; I'd rather be in the orphanage than be around him."

Still making our way through the binder I brought, I hand her the postcard showcasing the kitchen with Leon's stamped contact information on the back.

"*Wow,* Evelyn kept everything, didn't she?"

I smile. "Yes."

"That looks like something I would help him hand out at those home-and-garden-type exhibitions. He'd take me out there to give people pamphlets for those Jalousie windows his company was installing, I do remember that."

She shares her memories with such clarity and candor. I continue listening intently and do my best to process all the information.

"His addiction or mental illness or maybe both just made him do crazy things. He'd just throw food off the table, he'd try to steal our own furniture...well, he did steal Sylvia's college money. He'd make our mother pay him to drive her to her job. And when he had to pay child support, he would pick up receipts off the ground. People had dropped them in the grocery store or the parking lot and he turned them in like he bought all those groceries for us."

In addition to the emotional and mental trauma, she experienced her share of physical abuse as well.

"He once almost broke my jaw. I tried to call our mom while she was away, and he ripped the phone right out of the wall and punched me."

I wince as she runs down her list of woundings like a list someone would share of their many travels over the years—this isn't the first time she's talked about each one. I know each sister has a list of their own, just like Dad and the siblings he grew up with, and I'm overwhelmed at the thought of all of their childhoods being filled with dozens of heartbreaking moments. Even so, they grew into resilient and compassionate adults.

Linda continues.

"But there were weekends we would have company...like the Lawrentzes... he wouldn't act as crazy. We'd have a couple chickens, mashed potatoes, and noodles...then Sylvia and I would sing while we did all the dishes after one of those get-togethers. He could really fool people and be really charming. He was very intelligent—our mother told us we got our smarts from him. I can't remember what, but he even invented stuff to attach to the ping pong table that he put down in the basement. He was a big Cleveland Indians fan, so during the summer he'd have the transistor radio on to tune in to the games."

I'd like to think they could relax when he had some calm and "normal" moments. But it may have been a relief similar to walking in a minefield when you haven't yet stepped on a mine.

"So did he have any other health issues in his life aside from the addiction and possible bipolar disorder?"

"Oh he had ulcers and bad teeth—he got false teeth early." Linda starts to crack up as another story comes to mind. "He took us on this small roller coaster after he had gotten those false teeth... well... he laughed and the teeth flew right out of his mouth!" We giggle together.

The stories and memories flow freely. I want to stay as long as Linda and I are comfortable on these restaurant chairs and as long as the wait staff are friendly with us. I keep an eye on their faces as they continue to refill our water and ask if we need anything else. "No, thank you," I say, and then, "I'm sorry if we're taking too long—"

"Oh, no, no, no!" says the friendly server, who I get the feeling could be the owner, and she points to the still-open photo album on the table.

"Is this you?" she asks.

I am not sure who she's referring to but seeing that our story was by no means a short one, I stick with a short answer. I point to the picture I think she's referring to with the Lawrentz siblings as kids.

"Well, that is my dad and some family…my dad is her brother," I explain as I nod toward Linda. We are just a normal family.

"Oh, that is so nice," insists the server, "take your time visiting, no rush."

As we settle back into Linda's memories, I ask her if she recalls a woman named Frances McDonald from around that same time frame.

"I don't know. He was having an affair with a redhead across the street at Ridge Road in Mansfield, that coulda been her or another woman, too." She thinks. "As for the duffle bag full of stuff, I did hear that he had a disguise when he'd try to pull something off. There were wigs and a nylon stocking, I guess for over his face. He used Sylvia's white church gloves, too."

She pauses and says quietly, "Sometimes I think: who all has he murdered?" I'm struck by her comment and am silent. Part of me could believe he was capable, but on the other hand, I think even with all the things Leon did, could he have really gone that far? Did the violence directed towards his family spill over to people outside of the family who happened to get in his way? I think about the accidental bullet wound in his leg and the two guns and ammo in his duffle bag. Was it the first time he had packed such a bag? So he accidentally shot himself in the leg, *or* some unknown person shot him—but he couldn't explain any of it to the police without possibly incriminating himself. Maybe he told Mabee.

I also can't decide if Leon being armed in the first place was to defend himself from any gambling trouble, to intimidate, or if there had been something more nefarious.

As we finish up our tea and our conversation, Linda sighs. "People had to keep *so* many secrets, didn't they?"

CHAPTER 25

SHORTY

Early Fall, 2019

"They tunnel through the rock;
their eyes see all its treasures.
They search the sources of the rivers
and bring hidden things to light."
JOB 28:10-11

"Uncovering all this—it's too fascinating for you to quit!" Mae and I sit around her small kitchen table once again. It's been over two years since Dad and I took her out for lunch to give her the scoop. Of course, we had chatted a few times in between then and now, but with proof still finding me, I want to give her an update and see if she has any fresh takes on the situation.

"One thing that doesn't sit well, though—all this is coming out and she's not here to defend herself or explain things."

"I know," I say. "I wonder what she would have had to say about it all. I hope she'd be relieved to know we would still love her, and not judge her."

Mae nods. "Phil was enough to drive anyone to bed with someone else! When I stop and think about it, I hope her liaison with Leon—I hope it gave her a little bit of joy, because she was going through hell—"

179

she interrupts herself, a bit incredulous, "and as close of friends as we were, I can't believe I never knew about him! I still don't know how that happened! —Well, she was obviously good at keeping a secret!"

I ask her if she thinks Grandma also kept the secret from Phil. Did she think he knew about the affairs—particularly Leon? From what I observed and what family stories were shared, it seemed like there wasn't anything that would have made Phil doubt that Mike and Frank were not his sons. Mae isn't sure he would've caught on.

"Back in those days, when you got married, you (as the woman) kind of gave up your life. And your husband was the boss of the family," Mae explains. I wonder how both she and Grandma would have experienced life if their husbands went against the grain of society and truly saw them as equals. I glance at the new pictures I brought with me to show her.

"Mae, I was thinking about all of Grandma's pictures—she took so many, but there are a bunch that she's actually posing in from high school up until a time before my dad was born. She seemed to have more self-esteem then." I point to a few photos I've always admired.

"I have some of myself posed like these," she grins, remembering. "Both our guys were in the service, so this is what you did when they were gone. You sent them glamour shots as if to say 'Ha! See what you're missing?'" I smile.

"Was it normal to take as many pictures as Grandma did throughout her life then?"

"No...you had to be interested in photography. My mother was crazy with a camera, so I picked up the hobby. That's what rubbed off on Evelyn. And she took a lot!"

I knew Grandma's brother Harold (our Uncle Buzz), was an avid cameraman, but I didn't realize Mae and her mother were also influences in Grandma's photographic interests. Grandma wasn't financially well-off at any point in her life, so I ask Mae if it was expensive to buy film and develop pictures as much as she did. Mae attests that it was actually a very affordable hobby to have. She pauses. "There were parts of her life she wanted to preserve in her own mind, so she took pictures...and now you're finding them."

The last thing I want to show Mae during our visit is a letter. I was surprised to find something *so* personal, but I wasn't shocked my grandma stashed it away with all the other treasures. The letter was written by Evelyn's dad (my great-grandpa) Frank. In mid-August of 1966, during the height of the turmoil in the Lawrentz family, the divorce from Phil was final and she and Pete were together.

> *"Dear LaRue, Please don't throw this letter away until you have read it. Mom and I are both worried sick because we can't hear from you and don't know how to get in touch with you if it should be necessary. It seemed that you did not want us to know where you were moving or were afraid to trust us.*
>
> *I know you are hurt to the core and have a right to be. I don't want you to go through life hating us and perhaps causing the children to hate us. Now if I have hurt your feelings please forgive me. I really didn't think about you moving so soon. I kept calling and got no answer. I went by and you had moved out, so please try to get in touch with us and let us know how you are.*
>
> *We're not going to send anyone out to see you and especially Phil. I don't hate him but I hope I never see him anymore. When he walked out on his own flesh and blood it showed him for the man he was. When I told him about the incident in Shelby he didn't deny it and said you may as well have put it in the newspaper. I'll hush by saying please try to let us hear from [you].*
>
> *Love, Dad and Mom"*

"Well, I'll be darned!" Mae says, reacting to the emotionally charged letter. Pete had already moved Grandma and the kids out to the place on Bailey Lakes before they were married in October. She had been cut off from her family and friends. It was likely Pete's choice, but the newly single mom of four seemed to go along with it all the same given her vulnerable state. I don't know that I wouldn't have done the same, given the era and the circumstances.

"I cried a lot because I couldn't get in touch with her," Mae laments, "It was like losing part of yourself. When Pete took the family away, it worried me how he was treating her. 'Cause back then he was an alcoholic—he was a drunk! Very possessive...he didn't want to share the family with anybody. I remember when Evelyn finally said, 'It's the drink or me!' And thank heavens he did give it up. But it was kind of a secret life. He was terrible until he turned nice."

I thought about the ultimatum story that circulated around our family explaining how Grandpa Boreman quit drinking and smoking cold turkey. As if a magic spell was broken one day, with a skillet to the head. Maybe there is truth to that story after all.

"Do you remember how they even met?" I ask.

"I really can't...but I do remember he had been cheated on, but he also cheated on his first wife. And then after he met Evelyn, he came on to me. Twice!"

Mae is full of surprises, isn't she?

"The first time was before they were married, and the second time was after they were married. He called me at work and wanted to take me out to dinner. I really read him the riot act, 'cause he was married—they were married! I told him, 'If you forget you ever made this telephone call, I'll forget it, too.'"

While I know he was not the ideal marriage partner when he was an alcoholic, I feel like that was an awful line to cross, even when drunk. Mae was her best friend. But then again, Leon had presumably approached Grandma; I just haven't figured out if it was before or after she became friends with Wilma. Truth doesn't always mesh with memories, but somehow our memories end up being the God's honest truth as far as the individual is concerned.

We wrap up our time together and even through all of Mae's graciousness in humoring my incessant questions, I also know it's a reminder of the friend she's now without.

"I had a friend who passed a couple years ago, but when we'd talk on the phone, I would call her Evelyn (in my mind). It was hard to replace your grandmother. And when you get to be my age, you just don't have many close friends anymore. They are all gathering up there, waiting for me. I keep telling Him I'm ready but He's not listening."

⚜

Donald Jr. Boreman, or Pete, as friends called him, was the son of farmers from Congress, Ohio. Hard work and hard upbringing made him a hard man. Alcohol didn't help the short-fused fella but he loved my grandma and let her buy all the junk her heart desired from Goodwill and yard sales. He lovingly called her "Shorty" though he wasn't much taller than she was. They seemed dependent on each other, for better or worse. He really couldn't do much without her by his side and she couldn't drive, so anywhere they went, they went together.

When he was a young man, and before they were married, he worked at a sawmill. One day, his left-hand glove got stuck on the conveyor belt. As Grandpa recalled, the 'drunken idiots' wouldn't shut off the conveyor even though he yelled for them to stop. His four fingers went right through that blade, and when he pulled off the work glove, he had only his thumb left.

Dad remembers getting smacked in the rear end with that "stub." He said it hurt worse than just a regular old hand. The loss of four digits didn't seem to faze Pete. He owned and operated a body repair shop and was as hard-working of a mechanic as they come.

Neither stub nor hand ever smacked us out of anger or discipline, but I do remember some "birthday spankings" when we were younger kids. Always one more than we were old. "One to grow on," he would say. I could tell he was rough around the edges, but he showed a soft side to his granddaughters.

He joked with us and called us "boys" when we'd get to their house for a visit, usually having just put down a Louis L'Amour western or letting the credits of a John Wayne movie continue to scroll up their TV screen.

He would frequently open his wallet to show us a crisp new $100 bill, our eyes became wide with disbelief. When we'd least expect it, he'd pop his bottom row of dentures out of his mouth to get a rise out of us. He loved taking us to Mom's Family Restaurant, known for their hamburgers, and Arby's. We'd never go to McDonald's because he swore up and down they served kangaroo meat. The best ice cream came from Dairie Dolly, but when we stayed at their house and weren't going out for dessert, a gallon-sized bucket o' ice cream was always in their freezer—sometimes chocolate, sometimes Neapolitan. Perhaps nestled against the Blizzard of '78 snowball Grandma kept.

Pete loved assigning nicknames. In addition to Grandma being "Shorty," he called my dad "High Pockets" as he was growing up. I was "Miss America" as a little girl, bad drivers everywhere were "stupid idiots," and most of the local college students were "damn hippies" (but only when he remembered they existed) when we passed by the campus in his '88 Oldsmobile.

On the back addition of their house on Pearl Street he tended to climbing roses. Posing with pride beside them, Grandma would snap a photo every so often when they were looking especially regal.

Grandpa Boreman was at every birthday party and came to many of our school activities, even if he consistently left early, completely missing the last few songs, scenes, or innings we performed or played in. "Shorty, let's go. We'll beat the traffic."

But back in the summer of 1966, cruel spirited men and the continual battle of making ends meet made it a chaotic time for Grandma and the kids. Only a first grader, Dad was hospitalized for an ulcer. The preacher from their church had come to the house to make sure Grandma knew it was displeasing to God to get a divorce from her husband. I always thought that it was a clean break between Phil and finding Pete but obviously because of the records I discovered, I knew that wasn't true.

One day in 1967, Phil had paid someone to jump Pete and beat him up as he walked back from work. I'm sure that put ol' Petermo through the roof. He had had enough. But he hadn't had enough to drink yet. He continued drinking and showing violent behavior toward Evelyn and the kids. Ripping a phone out of the wall and not allowing them to play with neighbor kids were only a taste of the offenses.

In a pile of legal papers kept, I found some of the ones between Grandma and Phil from 1966. Amused, I smiled. Of course she had them. She bested me again and saved the very records I thought I needed to dig up at the court house that day in 2017.

But there was a set of documents from 1967 I hadn't laid eyes on before and wouldn't have known to search for at the courthouse. A Summons in Action for Divorce, an Order of Injunction, a Notice of Application for Temporary Alimony, and the Petition for Divorce between her and *Pete*. Did my family know about this?

"Summons and Order: 9 September 1967 / Court Date for Hearing on Alimony: 16 September 1967

> *... Donald J. Boreman, 534 West Main Street, Ashland, Ohio... Evelyn Boreman has filed in the office of the Clerk of the Court of Common Pleas of Ashland... asking that she be divorced from him and that she receive alimony...*
>
> *By an order of this Court... you are enjoined from coming onto the home premises occupied by the Plaintiff and her children, or any premises occupied by the Plaintiff and her children, and that he further be enjoined from annoying her and her children off of the premises during the pendency of this action and until final hearing of this cause.*
>
> *... Plaintiff and Defendant were married October 9, 1966, at Winchester, Virginia, and no children were born issue of this marriage.*
>
> *The Defendant has been guilty of gross neglect of duty and extreme cruelty, the particulars of which are well known to the Defendant and by reason of which the parties are no longer able to live together as husband and wife.*
>
> *Plaintiff further alleges that the Defendant has struck and beat her and has threatened to kill her and that unless he be restrained from coming onto the premises occupied by the Plaintiff and from annoying her and her children, she fears for the safety of her children and herself."*

I was proud of her for going to such lengths, but also felt her shame. Was she thinking, *I was just here last year to get away from Phil, and now this?*

The petition for divorce was clearly dropped in time for their first anniversary; the marriage would go on to last 35 years until Grandpa passed away in March of 2001. Throughout all the hardships of their marriage, I know she loved him, and he loved his "Shorty" back.

In the early 2000s, disposable cameras became popular, and Grandma always kept one handy, just as she would cough drops in her purse. At his calling hours, she brought one to snap a photo or two of him in his casket and of course to capture the many beautiful flower arrangements sent by their family and friends. They were surrounded by roses.

CHAPTER 26

LONESOME JOURNEY
Fall, 2019

With the holiday season not far off, the family gatherings were in full swing. It's the second Sunday in a row we get to enjoy time with Kaj and his daughter, Anna.

It's a remarkable opportunity to connect with these relatives from Sweden. Kaj's mother (Anna's namesake), is Grandpa Carl Eckstrom's younger sister. He is Leon's first cousin, despite the twenty-two year age difference.

The week prior, we all gathered for some homestyle fare at an Amish-kitchen buffet halfway between Ashland and Columbus. Occupying a large section of the restaurant (and occasionally playing an unintentional game of musical chairs) we needed an extra-long table and a waitress with extra-long patience. Only the large table was available for our visit. But for today's get together, our large Viking troop invades Jen's house for pictures, stories, and food.

Kaj is doing a wonderful job speaking English, and when he occasionally gets stuck, Anna is able to help translate. We spend time in the living room watching Debbie's slideshow of her trips to Sweden, and Kaj weighs in on places and people he recognizes.

Around Jen's dining room table, pictures and old letters fill the space as our

Swedish cousins translate words written long ago to Carl, from his mother (Kaj's grandmother) Hildur. This old world before four Ekström brothers immigrated to the United States is fascinating. And the world that continued there through World Wars and post-war equally amazes me.

Many of the photos and letters are from an antique steamer trunk Debbie brought from her house for today's gathering.

We open it, anticipating wild and exceptional discoveries. The trunk has seen better days, but still holds its historic transatlantic charm. It's painted partly black, with the bare areas revealing dark-stained wood. A metal clasp keeps the box lid locked and closed. Adorned with a few ornate details and bonus buckles, it is the same piece of luggage Carl Eckstrom used to start his new life in America.

With all his belongings packed up, he boarded a large ship and arrived at Ellis Island on August 5, 1914. A postcard from the ship had been placed in the steamer trunk as a keepsake. As I look over the 105 year old paper card, I notice how the center, woven in silk, shows an American flag and a Swedish flag above two arms extended in a handshake with the phrase "Hands Across the Sea: RMS *Olympic.* "

Since I was eleven, I desperately wanted to be related to someone who had been on the *Titanic*. Now, I was waltzing right into claiming my great-grand-father as a third-class passenger on the sister ship of the infamous and ill-fated vessel. Thank God he wasn't on the *Titanic* two years earlier—as a steerage passenger the chances of survival were horrifically slim. The reality is both Carl and his future that included all of us could have been lost in the North Atlantic.

In the trunk are more loose photos, letters, yellowed newspapers, knickknacks, old worn leather wallets, manuals to appliances, small household items, receipts, important documents, some loose pictures, and a scrapbook full of pictures.

In this scrapbook a clipping of a poem "To Helen" was pasted next to a picture of Leon's parents, Carl and Helen. It looked as if someone took an X-ACTO knife down the middle of the two figures in the photo and tried to peel Carl's side out. However, the adhesive was strong. I guess the person trying to tear him out gave up.

As my family chats and pours over the items, I decide I should just start documenting. I pull my phone out from my purse and take pictures of each piece that slides in front of my view, set it aside, and move on to the next.

A gold mine of photos from southern Sweden and Davenport, Iowa, from the twenties and thirties. Then postcards to Mansfield written by a seven-year-old Leon and six-year-old Carl Jr. to their dad when they were (presumably with their mother) away visiting family in Chicago.

"Dear Daddy, Thank you for the nice cards. Send us some more. We are very lonesome for you. We are going to bed now. Goodnight Daddy. From, Leon and Carlie"

As we dig through the trunk's contents, we pull out a newspaper from 1980: "Kinda-Posten: Nyhets-och annonstidning for Kinda och Ydre härader." A mallet, a brass coffee urn or a tea kettle, maybe. A National brand Order Book (an accounting ledger book). A Western Union Telegram. B&W cigarette papers. And a wooden box with Lily White Grade A Gloucester Style Codfish branded by Slade Gorton & Co. painted on its top.

There is another wooden box though, polished and smooth, with a little brass latch on the side that keeps the lid closed. Inside is a Memorial Bible, like some kind of keepsake Bible a funeral home would give to the family of a deceased loved one after the service. It's blinding white with what looks like Easter lilies debossed on the front. A zipper is keeping the Bible shut tight, all the way around the top, down the side, across the bottom.

I start to unzip the cover, and its slightly tarnished metal teeth catch, and I cringe. Carefully, I manage to unzip the rest without pinching my fingers or prolonging the irritating metallic scratching sound. I lock in on the first page which provides an elaborate decorative section for personalization.

The prompts were "Presented in loving memory of" and "by" with a place for a date. It is all filled with mostly capital letters in blue ink that was starting to run out.

53 YEARS OF "LONELINESS"
STARVED FOR TRUE LOVE & UNDERSTANDING
Presented in Loving Memory of

LEON "GUSTAV" EKSTROM • 2-7-23 THRU 5-31-76
by HIS "MOM & DAD" HELEN AND CARL H.
Date: 5-30-76
(I'M UPSTAIRS WITH THE MAN, PRAY FOR ME)

The din of the family around me continues. *What on earth am I staring at?* I look up from the Bible and make eye contact with Jen and motion for her to follow me. Once in the kitchen, I plop the holy yet kind of disturbing book on the counter.

"What did you find?" Jen asks. I pass her the open Bible as we quietly discern what we're looking at. "He died in 1999, so that's obviously not his actual death date," she reasons.

"Why would they keep this in the trunk? Or keep it at all?" I wonder out loud.

Disconcerted, Jen responds, "Who knows? So bizarre…"

"For a second I thought it was some weird way to disown Leon as a son, but now that I think about it…he must have written it himself."

"Yes, it has to be," Jen nods, "My mom said he always wrote in all capital letters."

"My dad writes that way, too," I say.

I turn the page. I thought the first part would have been the only page with writing, but another whole page was filled out. This time the date is 5-26-76, which is at the top and the bottom of the page. It's the "Presented to" page and even more decorative than the first page, this time with blue, gold, reddish colors in the design surrounding the commemorative text.

Presented to:
MY MOTHER & DAD, HELEN MATILDA & CARL HENRY by
SON "LEON GUSTAV" & WILMA ADELAIDE
Date 5-26-76

I'm not sure if we'll ever know the full story about what happened or didn't happen between May 26th through Memorial Day weekend, 1976. Or why Wilma's name was written with his.

CHAPTER 27

MERCY STREET

November, 2019

Helen & Carl Eckstrom

> *TO HELEN*
>
> *All is mute and drear*
> *Silenced the sound my heart would hear,*
> *Helen's laughter, soft and clear.*
> *My heart took up each silken note;*
> *In my memory they still float.*
> *Helen, if you can forgive,*
> *And forgiving, let me live.*
> *Trill the magic song of yore,*
> *O Helen, laugh for me once more.*
> *GEORGE, THE MAN WITH A PAST.*

(This poem comes from a clipping pasted at the front of an old photo
album of the Eckstrom family from the 1920s; author unknown.)

"SURPRISE!" We shout and start singing the happy birthday tune.
Someone adds "EARLY!" after each "Happy." It's not December yet, but
to throw him off the scent and to avoid scheduling challenges over the

holidays, Dad's surprise party had been planned for November.

We set up for a couple hours and my shoes were already off, so at the end of the song, I hurry up to him and stand on my bare tippy toes to give him a hug and a kiss on the cheek. All three of his girls are here. His wife of 38 years. His grandkids, sons-in-law, an uncle and aunt, nephew, brother-in-law and sister-in-law, high school friends, long time family friends, both brothers, and three of his "new" sisters.

His "birthday twin" Karen holds a 60th birthday balloon with him as we take their picture. Susie, Linda, Frank, and Jim talk and share stories of childhood and the recent events that brought us all together. Five decades of photos pile up on a nearby card table.

I think about Grandma and wish she was here to enjoy the celebration. Soon the year will come to an end, and she'll have been gone for ten years. Peggy Lee's warm voice covers me like a blanket as I hear her sing the chorus of *My Dear Acquaintance* once more.

The event room at the Community Center is filled with voices and Dad's favorite songs as he makes his way around the room, smiling and laughing, thanking people for coming and feeling celebrated and loved by all the wonderful people he's crossed paths with throughout his 60 years all together in one space.

He is a man with a past.

Dad's Surprise 60th Birthday Party
Back L-R: Elizabeth, Jim, Mike, Frank, Allison; **Front L-R:** Susie, Karen, Samantha, Linda

Back in 2012, we had our daughter, Clementine LaRue. Grandma didn't get to meet her, but her namesake seemed to get some of her best and quirkiest qualities. In her smile, her bare feet, her love of nature and animals, snapping pictures with her Instax camera; in each bit there is a piece of Evelyn LaRue. Plus, if I had believed in reincarnation, this would have caused me a fair amount of alarm: I caught her inspecting the trash in the kitchen the other day. The scrap paper and cloth I tossed in, she explained, were still good—she could "make something with it." *Okay, Evelyn,* I mused.

Grandma told me her name meant "Hazelnut" and with her middle name LaRue, meaning "The Street" she was Hazelnut Street, which I thought was funny because she had lived on a nut street: Walnut. In other derivations, Evelyn also means "longed-for child" and "light." I think about my great-grandparents and their struggle at first to have a child and wonder if her name had something to do with their three lost babies.

With Miles, it's a French form of Michael. The German and Irish origin means "soldier or servant" and the English version it means "merciful."

When we decided on Clementine, it was picked because it was unique and just felt right. We read about its meaning as an afterthought. One of the meanings of Miles happened to be the same as Clementine's: Merciful. That settled it for us. It was perfect. We hope our children will experience the mercy and forgiveness God shows us as well as offering mercy, grace, generosity, compassion, and forbearance to others in return. I wish Grandma could have met our little red-headed Mercy Street.

As time passed, more stories hidden in the larger family were revealed. Three of the Eckstrom sisters' children each found a half-brother, just like their mothers found a long-lost brother in my dad.

What was "secret" and "hidden" in our story has been brought into the open, into the light. I think I'll always have more questions, and we may not fully understand all of it, but I can say I've witnessed God take something that was meant for harm and watch him redeem it for good.

I'm reminded how most people are left with nothing tangible when they find out a secret like this. Nothing to prove there was an event or a relationship in the past. Nothing but some DNA.

Things were destroyed, sold off, thrown out by relatives trying to keep their loved ones from being on the next episode of *Hoarders*. And there were times my family were those people and are those people.

There are the hoarders and the "get-rid-of-it" types. My grandma may have classified as a hoarder if you had to put her in a box. But she was a record keeper.

A keeper of the things that mattered to her, things that might matter to someone else. The ultimate collection of proof that she lived and proof of the events that happened to her even when she couldn't remember them in the end.

My own childhood autograph book held notable signatures from the likes of Santa, the Tooth Fairy, and the Easter Bunny. Of course it also had signatures and notes from friends, my sisters, my parents, and grandparents. On the very last page is my grandma's "signature" to me:

> *"By hook or by crook,*
> *I'll be the last to write in your book."*
> *- Grandma B.*

And so she is.

A GHOST STORY

(for the record)

I first heard about the haunted tunnel when I was a teenager. Every town has one. It may not be a tunnel, per se, but all places have an urban legend (or in this case small-town legend) of some haunted location that newly licensed teenagers drive to for excitement on a Friday night after a football game. One of Ashland's was the "haunted tunnel."

Much like my love for family history, my fascination with the supernatural (with a concentration in ghosts) also started young. In fact, I was a founding member of "The Ghost Mystery Club," or as we liked to refer to it, the GMC. Three girlfriends and I loved watching *Unsolved Mysteries,* reading R.L. Stine and the *Scary Stories* series. We checked out books at the school and public libraries about poltergeists, ESP, real-life haunted places, and the historical tragedies preceding these hauntings.

Naturally, as fourth and fifth graders, we scared easily. Hearing about Bloody Mary on the bus ride home from school and the subsequent attempt to try it in the bathroom mirror was the extent of my summoning spirits, but the excitement of learning about places thought to be haunted and the real stories connected to them continued with me to adulthood.

Our haunted tunnel was out in the country, and since I am a self-pro-claimed directionally challenged person, "out in the country" was all I knew about its location. I had always been a passenger the couple of times driving through with friends. As for the story behind the haunted label attached to it, an actual historical incident has never materialized as far as I know.

Directions for experiencing said haunt: Travel on the road that goes under this railroad bridge; pull fully inside the tunnel and turn off your lights; put the vehicle in neutral and wait. Ghosts will push you one way or the other out of the tunnel, and you may even see their handprints if your car is dirty enough. It's an old looking stone tunnel and bridge, but since the invention of spray paint, it tends to be a bit more colorful than when it was first constructed. Spoiler alert: What they fail to tell you as a wide-eyed jumpy teen is about the slight incline on that strip of road directly inside the tunnel. Still, I dare you to drive down there alone at night, even if you're the most skeptical of mature adults.

When Jason and I were first married and bought our first home that summer on Banning Avenue, we had a house-warming party with a few friends. A friend and co-worker at the design company I worked for brought us an original photo of his, matted and framed. With our mutual interest in the supernatural, I wasn't surprised the house-warming gift he gave us was of the infamous haunted tunnel. We loved it.

*

It's 2018 and already one year into our life-altering discovery, but there is a stand-still regarding the paper trail on "the old man." I turn my attention to the woman named in the newspaper as being connected with Leon's forgery case.

The blonde wig, the one forged check signed by a mysterious "Elsie Dildomedes" ...this had to be Frances McDonald's supporting actress role in the show. Between my own research and the help of my friend Jayson, I came to learn that Frances was married to a man named Jerry McDonald, but they had become estranged.

Over the years, Frances worked in a few places I recognized: T&A Saveway and Lumberman's Mutual Insurance. Her charges in the forgery case had been dropped by the county prosecutor and *"the grand jury indictment against her was canceled,"* reads the notice in the February 17, 1960 edition of the *Mansfield News Journal.* Frances still had a Mansfield address, but a year prior (in 1959) Jerry was living in Ashland. Hopping through records, I notice an occasional address in Mansfield, but it seemed to be the location of his son's home, or of the service station where he and his son both worked.

As I continue the search for more about Frances, I see a legal notice in the *Mansfield News Journal* from February 27, 1960, stating that *"... Frances McDonald, 138½ Grasmere Avenue, Mansfield, Ohio has been duly appointed and qualified as Administratrix in the estate of Jerry L. McDonald, deceased, late of Mansfield, Richland County, Ohio. Date: February 19, 1960."*

"You've got to be kidding me", I mutter to myself. She was cleared of charges of forgery and then just a couple days later, she's qualified as executor of her estranged husband's estate?

Because suddenly he was dead.

At 41 years of age.

Nope, did not expect that. I put my research of Frances aside and focus on Jerry. After a quick search on *Newspapers.com,* I find what I'm looking for.

"Ashlander Dies In Blaze: Falls Through Hole Burned In Floor."

In the October 14, 1959 edition of the *Mansfield News Journal* it's front-page news. I read, eagerly scanning the text to find out exactly how he met his end.

"...investigating the death of Jerry Lewis McDonald, 41, late yesterday in a fire in his home on Ashland County Road 52, about three miles southwest of Ashland. Fire damage to the two-story frame house was confined to a large hole in the floor of one room. Sheriffs deputies said McDonald, who had just been released from the hospital where he had been undergoing treatment for ulcers, apparently was lying on the davenport, got up and fell through a hole the fire had burned in the

floor. McDonald's body was found over the coal furnace pipes below the room damaged by the blaze...

The victim reportedly had come home and started a fire in the furnace before lying down..."

Horrified, I realize the only reason I am reading about Jerry McDonald perishing over a burning furnace was because his estranged wife had a criminal connection (allegedly) with my grandfather.

I go over my timeline. Leon was writing bad checks on September 8, 1959, in Mansfield, then on September 13th and 14th in Ashland. Leon's not arrested until October 30 in the Bucyrus apartment. (Recall the infected bullet wound and a duffle bag full of goodies incident.) Frances was also arrested in connection with the forgery scheme—from what I can tell at least based on the September 13th check signed by "Elsie," though her employment at T&A Saveway (in addition to Lumberman's) in Mansfield also gives me suspicion about that fake check made out to that very store for cash on September 8th.

Ironically, an article in the *Mansfield News Journal* from September 25th announces, "Fire Prevention Week Plans Readied" for the week of October 4th, hosted by Lumberman's Mutual Insurance agency. Then, there is a September 29th hospital admission mentioned in the *Mansfield News Journal* for Jerry's ulcers, so that checks out.

Fall weather in Ohio is like any other season in Ohio—a surprise. Northeast Ohio had been enjoying the upper 60's the first week and a half of October in 1959, but the forecast from Monday, October 12th showed a dip in temperature. *"It's Wintry—The Mansfield area today got a taste of what's to come... more rain tomorrow night and Wednesday. Lows tonight will be in the thirties and some frost is likely. The five-day forecast calls for readings five to seven degrees below normal."*

Jerry had been admitted to the hospital while temperatures were in the high-60s/ low-70s only to be released back to a two-story house just southwest of Ashland during a cold front. From all accounts, he seemed to live alone, and that coal furnace would have needed to be lit to get the house all warmed up so he could recoup comfortably.

I feel bad that my thoughts are already implicating Leon, as scheming and calculating as he was, in having a role in Jerry's demise. There is no proof at all—just a connection with the guy's wife that could have nothing to do with anything. Still, I want to learn every detail I can about the incident.

The digitized *Mansfield News Journal* is a scanned blessing of research material I have from the comfort of my couch when I spend late nights researching. But this fire happened in Ashland County on County Road 52, "three miles southwest of the city of Ashland." Wherever that was. Road names and numbers have since changed so a Google maps search leaves me scratching my head. I decide I need to go to the Ashland Public Library and at least see if the incident is mentioned in the *Ashland Times-Gazette.*

The first chance I get, we drive over to the library. I send the kids with Jason to Juvenile and I make my way to the second floor where the microfilm machines live, bounding up the steps two at a time. I know I'll get distracted and take too long, and my family will not have patience for that without some kind of frozen dairy bribery. If I must suffer the consequences, so be it.

With the machines all to myself, I put my bag down on a chair, throw open the metal file cabinet with the right decade of film boxes and select the one labeled Oct-Dec 1959.

I feed the film through the winding gears and start dialing forward. After a short whirr of the microfiche, I stop close enough to mid-October and inch forward slowly.

There.

October 14th.

Front page news, just like the *Mansfield News Journal,* only with additional details. And a picture.

"FIRE MARSHAL INVESTIGATING DEATH OF JERRY L. MCDONALD"

The photograph shows a group of men: the sheriff supervising (stogie hanging from his lips), two toward the house watching as the deputy sheriff and three others carry a body bag on a stretcher.

❧

When we moved at the end of the summer of 2018, we chose our new house because it wasn't much larger than our old one, but had ten times more land. Plenty of room to play wiffle ball, have bonfires, plant big gardens, hang disc swings from great old trees, and sled down the perfect hill.

While waiting for the sale to go through, we made a ritual out of driving by the house and exploring the back country roads that surrounded it. Since it's a corner lot, the house faces the main highway but the driveway is on a township road. If you continue down the hill about a half mile, over the railroad tracks, there's a farm that specializes in maple syrup, honey, apple cider, and blueberries. The best kind of people you'll meet in Ashland run that sweet place. From there you'll curve right around the bend, and at that point there's a fork in the road. Turning left keeps you on the same township road. Or, if you go straight and to the right you'll end up on a smaller county road that continues on just over a mile and wraps back around to the main highway. It comes out by a couple residences and then soon to the left is a small brick building that's home to a local battery business.

The first time we explored back here after our offer was accepted for the house, I was taken aback. Down this short back road were tall maples with syrup lines winding around their trunks and connecting through wooded acres, here and there a couple of small clearings—a meadow or a field of feed corn. After passing an old farmhouse, there is a quick bend in the road and you are abruptly met with an old stone tunnel bridge layered in graffiti. Our friend's housewarming gift seemed prophetic. The haunted tunnel was practically in our new backyard.

❧

My Grandpa Scroggs had done genealogy and research the hard way. You go to libraries, you go to courthouses, you send away for records if you can't go there yourself to look them up. I began my family history obsession when the internet was still a fairly new thing to the average American and found myself overwhelmed by the number of records I had at my fingertips.

Although I had felt a little guilty about that, the advancement of technology is supposed to help make things faster and easier, so I didn't feel guilty for long. I realized it was a gift that I could share with my grandpa. Now I could contribute to research questions that had stumped him when the physical paper trail ended due to time, money, or distance.

However, just like the other times I needed to physically go to the courthouse or the library, I find myself back downtown, needing help with answers that had not been scanned and uploaded to all the databases I check. This time I'm in the courthouse basement. The maps office.

"I'm trying to figure out where Ashland County Road 52 would be in present day," I tell the clerk. "The article I saw the road referenced in was from 1959…and it mentioned it was three miles southwest of Ashland. If that's helpful…" I trail off.

He enters the info into his computer, looking carefully for my random request. A few results appear; he looks them over and then reaches to a shelf nearby and pulls out a map. Confident he has the right one, he places it on the counter in front of me so I can see.

"Okay, that was off of 42 going toward Mansfield." He points and runs his finger down the Route 42 line south. My stomach drops. "Okay… do you know where Ohio Battery is?" I nod, knowing exactly where Ohio Battery is.

"Well, you take a right on that first road, Township Road 1536. That was County Road 52 in 1959."

The 12-year-old in me squeaks out: "You mean the road where the haunted tunnel is?"

He smirks. "Yes, that one."

This whole story began with the East Walnut Street home that was in my proverbial backyard from where we last lived for the first twelve years of marriage. And that house turned out to have more significant meaning than just being the place my dad lived in when he was a baby. And now, this side story to my family saga shows yet another house of significance that is right down the road from where I live.

After some more help from my maps man and additional digging of the documents he printed out for me, I pinpoint the exact house that Jerry McDonald lived and died in. Currently inhabited, the home is set back down a gravel lane—and wouldn't you know, it's the house closest to that old, creepy tunnel.

As for the complete *Ashland Times-Gazette* article with additional details surrounding the fire incident:

"Mystery still surrounds the death of a 41-year-old Ashland County man who was found dead on the top of a coal furnace in the basement of his home at 6:05 p.m. Tuesday. Dead is Jerry Lewis McDonald, who lived on County Road 52 about one mile off U.S. 42 south of Ashland. The body is at Gilbert Funeral Home.

Coroner William H. Rower tentatively ruled the death "accidental" later this morning...

McDonald had built a fire in the furnace and had apparently laid down to take a nap on the living room couch.

Fire Chief Bernard Johnson said the house was closed up tight and no smoke was escaping when the fire was first discovered by some neighbors who had gone in the home to visit McDonald, home from the hospital only a few days...

Firemen rushed to the county home and possibly saved it from destruction. When they arrived, the two-story, six-room structure was full of smoke and a fire was blazing around the coal bin in the basement.

Johnson said he believed that the furnace overheated while Mr. McDonald was sleeping and that McDonald was dazed when he woke up and fell through the weakened floor above the furnace. This statement was backed up by Hower, who said he believed that McDonald was possibly under the influence of sedatives.

McDonald's car was parked at the home when the neighbors arrived to visit him. They were satisfied he was inside the home but the home was too hot to enter."

I gasp as I read the next line: *"Johnson said the house had recently been remodeled and had **new aluminum siding**…"*

How on earth am I supposed to ignore the fact that this guy's wife was in cahoots with Leon forging checks while his day job was working as a FRICKEN ALUMINUM SIDING SALESMAN? My head is spinning. The article continues:

"Surviving are McDonald's estranged wife Frances…"

I fill my parents in on these findings. Per usual they are intrigued and entertained by what I report, with my dad still in comical acceptance yet disbelief of the bizarre curve ball he'd been thrown in his late 50s.

Because they are familiar with the connection between Leon and Frances and knew of the Jerry McDonald story, I had another set of eyes keeping a lookout. After the NPE discovery, they knew enough of what to look for, and they were as entranced by the mystery and the secrets we were still uncovering as I was.

After hearing about the house location, my dad's eyes get wide. "You have to see this." He picks up a big book that leans against the end table next to his La-Z-Boy. It's a scrapbook. There were still a couple left from the very last bin of Grandma's keepsakes.

"I was leafing through this one Ali, and look—" He opens the bisque-colored scrapbook with a cartoonish 1950s young couple that look like they are going steady and heading off to a sock hop. A red-headed gal and a guy with a jet-black buzz cut sporting a blue and white polka dot bow tie. Dad flips to the back pages of the album and turns it around for me to see.

Now, you have to understand the kinds of things Evelyn LaRue Bowers Lawrentz Boreman liked to clip from newspapers and glue in her scrapbooks. We would call it click bait today. Honestly, things I would probably click on because I was curious, interested, or it made me laugh. She's doing the same. She's just pinning them on an old-fashioned Pinterest board.

This very scrapbook, for instance, has articles such as "In Hospital 66 Years" where a woman from Missouri had been admitted to a mental institution in 1893 when she was only 32 years old because of "simple melancholia" and 66 years later died there never having once received a visitor or a letter.

There is a clipping of three kittens who think a hen is their mother and nests with her, though the mom cat comes to feed them, and then leaves them with their adopted mother once again. The header is "Identity Crisis." Another title reads "Kitten with two heads" while still another is "Dead couple gets married."

And then there is this amusing yet problematic article title: "Housewife Just Rebels—Sets Fire To House: Drudgery Was Too Much So Pretty Wife Took Action." Some pages are dedicated to baby multiples being born, Siamese twin stories, and even one about a two-headed baby. She also has a whole page dedicated to stories in which people or things get struck by lightning.

But what my dad is showing me is something I've seen before. Once again, I had gone looking for something Grandma already had collected for me.

"FIRE MARSHAL INVESTIGATING DEATH OF JERRY L. MCDONALD"

The full article. Completely clipped out and pasted in *her* scrapbook with the *Ashland Times Gazette* header on top.

Then, the adjacent scrapbook page with three smaller columns of articles—all follow-ups from the McDonald story: "Probe Blaze That Killed Ashland Man," Jerry's full obituary, and finally "McDonald Death Accidental." Also clipped: the continuation of the story from page 16.

Grandma may as well have cut me out and pasted me on that struck-by-lightning page (I noticed there was a little room at the bottom right) because all the fine little hairs on my arms and on the back of my neck are now standing on end from the electric-like shock of what I'm seeing in this old scrapbook.

Whoever was connected to who and whatever happened or didn't happen that day in October of 1959 might *always* remain a mystery. The only surviving witnesses are nestled back in the woods, down the low-traffic country lane: the aging McDonald house and that old stone tunnel.

ABOUT THE AUTHOR

Allison Lawrentz Barnhart grew up in Ashland, Ohio, and graduated from Ashland University which included a year intensive at The Art Institute of Pittsburgh.

While working as a full-time graphic designer, she enjoys her life as a wife, mother, daughter, sister, cousin, friend, artist, gardener, and family historian. Genealogy research has been a constant love of hers since grade-school. With the encouragement of her amazing relatives on all sides of the tree, she has been on a decades long mission to not only build her own family's story and write about it, but to help others find joy in discovering their origins and tell their stories.

Allison resides in Ashland, Ohio, with her husband, two children, a rescue mini-dachshund, and an orange tabby they found in their garage one day.

www.ingramcontent.com/pod-product-compliance
Lightning Source LLC
Chambersburg PA
CBHW022051020426
42335CB00012B/639